HUME PAPERS ON PUBLIC POLICY:
Volume 5 No. 4

THE REFORM OF CIVIL JUSTICE

THE DAVID HUME INSTITUTE

HUME PAPERS ON PUBLIC POLICY:
Volume 5 No. 4

THE REFORM OF CIVIL JUSTICE

EDINBURGH UNIVERSITY PRESS

©David Hume Institute 1997

Edinburgh University Press
22 George Square, Edinburgh

Typeset in Times New Roman by WestKey Limited, Falmouth
and printed and bound in Great Britain
by Page Bros Limited, Norwich

A CIP record for this book is available from the
British Library

ISBN 0 7486 1123 1

Contents

Foreword	vii
An Economic Perspective on the Cost of Justice 　*Brian G. M. Main*	1
The Changing Landscape of Dispute Resolution 　*Richard Mays*	29
Fair Notice – The Role of Written Pleadings in the Scottish Justice System 　*Andrew Murray*	49
Judicial Case Management. The Quiet but Significant Revolution 　*Rachel Wadia*	66
Access to Justice? Lessons from the Sheriff Court 　*David Parratt*	96

Contributors

Brian G. M. Main is a Professor of Economics at the University of Edinburgh

Richard Mays is a Senior Lecturer in Law at The Robert Gordon University, Aberdeen

Andrew Murray is a Lecturer in Business Law at the University of Stirling

Rachel Wadia is a Researcher in the Faculty of Law at the University of Edinburgh

David Parratt is a Researcher in the Faculty of Law at the University of Edinburgh

Foreword

The efficient working of the justice system, particularly in terms of the general issue of access to justice, continues to be a topic of intense public policy discussion. In a recent issue of *Hume Papers on Public Policy* we examined aspects of legal aid and the organisation of the legal profession. We now return to the topic but this time with a collection of papers that focuses on the procedural arrangements that govern the progress of cases through the civil courts. Some of these considerations were previously visited in Hume Occasional Paper No. 43, *The Costs of Justice*, which published papers presented in 1993 at a Hume Conference sponsored by the Faculty of Advocates. Since that date, the publication of both Lord Woolf's report, *Access to Justice* (1995, 1996), and Lord Cullen's report, *Review of the Business of the Outer House of the Court of Session* (1996), has moved the debate along considerably by producing concrete proposals for reform in procedure in England and Wales and in Scotland, respectively.

The papers presented below are written in the context of the Scottish legal system but speak to the broader issues that arise when procedural reform is considered. Brian Main brings an economist's perspective to bear in asking what we expect from a system of civil justice. He argues that what is involved is a mechanism of dispute resolution. But this is a mechanism casting a very long shadow in the sense that it influences behaviour in alternative dispute resolution channels and even in activities where no dispute arises. This is because the existence of the court system provides a framework allowing parties to enter into mutually beneficial activities and contracts in the knowledge that, should a dispute arise, there exists a known and reliable way in which to resolve that dispute should other cheaper forms of dispute resolution fail. There is, therefore, a substantial positive externality generated by the court system that cannot be measured simply by considering those cases that appear in court. These benefits increase with the standard of accuracy of the courts, but, of course, accuracy comes at a price – more thorough and painstaking procedures for presenting evidence may lead to fewer 'mistakes' by the courts, but they will also slow the progress of cases down with the commensurate increase in delay and costs. Costs and decisions to persevere with complaints rather than settle are also influenced by the way litigation costs are allocated between the parties and the way in which lawyers are paid. A contrast is drawn here with arrangements in the USA.

The general thrust of the analysis presented in this paper is that there is certainly considerable scope for affecting the disposition of civil justice through procedural changes and there is also scope for allowing resources in the system to better reflect demand for the service (by increasing judicial capacity) and by further deregulating the legal profession. There will remain, however, a rather thorny issue of distributional justice in terms of access to justice by the poorer section of the population – access which would be eased with the introduction of fee arrangements such as the contingency fee but which is still likely to depend on public support through some form of legal aid.

The paper by Richard Mays offers an overview of some of the specific reforms proposed for the Court of Session and those that have already been implemented in the Sheriff Court. Substantial reform has already taken place in the Sheriff Court in terms of small claims and summary cause procedures. While open to criticism, these reforms are generally seen as a success and have made a clear impression on the reforms proposed for the Court of Session by Lord Cullen. Indeed, as Mays explains, the Court of Session has already experimented with procedural reform for commercial causes where a more interventionist approach of case management has been introduced. Mays also includes a detailed discussion of Alternative Dispute Resolution (ADR) and the role it has come to play in Scotland. There are those who regard ADR as a convenient labelling of something that has always taken place (e.g., arbitration or, even more widely, bargaining in the shadow of the law), but there is no doubt that the intermediate level of formality and the privately agreed procedural arrangements offer an attractive channel of dispute resolution to many commercial enterprises. In its most flexible variant, mediation, it offers a prospect of more enduring resolution to disputes involving family and relational matters where compliance and enforcement is a problem. There is a detailed discussion here of the state of arbitration law in Scotland and its relationship to that in England and Wales and to the more general model law proposed by the United Nations.

Mays concludes his paper with a review of the various dimensions of the civil justice system that are susceptible to reform: the adversarial nature of the system; delay; procedure; and case-management. This is done from the perspective that one can learn much about a society in terms of what it regards as just and fair from an examination of the practices and procedures adopted in its courts. The conclusion is that there is still a fair way to go as far as reform is concerned but that ADR mechanisms have an important role to play.

Andrew Murray considers in detail the system of written pleadings that characterises the Scottish system – variously regarded as the jewel in the crown or an Achilles' heel. A single document (the pleadings) comes to contain the detailed complaint of the pursuer in terms of the salient facts ('the condescendence') and the points in law upon which the case hangs ('pleas in law'). These are collectively known as 'the summons'. Also included in the pleadings is the response of the defender whereby facts that are not in dispute are admitted and challenges to the facts and arguments in law are laid out ('the defences'). In a process of interchanges between the parties the pleadings are refined. Each party is allowed to respond to the amendments of the other side ('adjustment') until the matter is laid out to the satisfaction, if not agreement, of both sides in what is known as 'the closed record'. The virtue of this system is that the judge is presented with what should be a very clear and focused picture of the dispute – reduced to its kernel. The purpose of the procedure is to narrow the dispute. It also avoids trial by ambush. Surprise is not meant to be a tactical weapon in the courtroom. But the path from the original summons to the appearance on court for proof can be a long one. Murray examines it in detail. To some it is a procedural minefield full of traps and unhelpful strategic manipulation of rules by the lawyers. To others it can be changed only at the cost of dulling the ability of the court to reach the correct decision.

Lord Cullen recommended reform of this system of pleadings. Reform has, in fact, been introduced in the Court of Session in the form of abbreviated pleadings under an optional procedure for personal injury claims. Murray discusses this innovation and the proposal by Lord Cullen to extend something similar to this procedure to all ordinary actions in the Court of Session, but is cautious regarding its utility in complex cases. In particular it may lead to an increased reliance on documentary evidence and the problems of discovery of evidence that arise in English courts. Transferring to more complex procedural tracks may only lead to higher costs and more delay. Vigorous case management is also seen as a threat to the accuracy of the case presented owing to the distance of the judge from the parties. Murray concludes that the existing system of pleading has more good points than bad, and enters a plea for professional responsibility among practitioners so that the existing system can be allowed to operate to its fullest advantage.

In a wide-ranging paper that draws on empirical research conducted in the Court of Session and elsewhere, Rachel Wadia reviews the recent history of civil justice in Scotland. The picture that emerges is of a system where costs are rising and delay is rife. A detailed review of current court practice in the Court of Session and the Sheriff Court is also presented, covering the system of case control, discharged hearings, pleadings, and court administration. A strong case is made for the need for reform, and it is pointed out that calls for reform have been voiced more and more loudly of late. The most recent contribution in this vein is, of course, the Cullen Review and it is upon this that Wadia concentrates. The particular aspect of the Cullen reform, and to many the most salient, is judicial case management. After reviewing some of the evidence from other jurisdictions where this has been implemented, Wadia presents an overview of the difficulties that would beset the introduction of such an approach into the Scottish legal system. Experience of difficulties encountered introducing earlier procedural reforms is detailed as a caution against over-optimism with regard to what can be achieved in the current Woolf/Cullen inspired round of case-management oriented reform proposals. But, on a more optimistic note, Wadia discusses the outcome of the recent pilot scheme introduction of case-management in the commercial cause actions of the Court of Session. This is generally seen as positive, but some difficulties are foreseen in terms of wider introduction of such an approach.

In the final paper in this collection, David Parratt takes a careful look at the lessons that can be learned from the recent experience of the Sheriff Court in introducing procedural reform. First, the weaknesses in the pre-reform (1993) system are discussed. These included unnecessary appearances in court, late filing of papers, last minute adjustments, and late settlements (at the door of the court). The 1993 reforms are then examined in terms of their robustness against such abuse. These rules set sharp time limits on the movement of a case towards trial and place the sheriff in a position to manage the progress of the case. It is argued that implementation has not been without its problems. This is due, in part, to the difficulty experienced by sheriffs in moving their practice from the old to the new rules, particularly in terms of becoming pro-active in case management. Changing rules may be easier than changing cultures. This is not made any easier by the strong collegiality that exists among lawyers, who are very tolerant of procedural mistakes made by opponents. An additional difficulty arises due to the decentralised nature of the sheriff court system, which is split into six sheriffdoms. Hence, although there was an extensive training programme for sheriffs in the new rules, it was easy for different (more indulgent) interpretations of these rules to emerge from sheriffdom to sheriffdom. These variations may well be transitory in nature, with a more standard practice emerging with the passage of time. The fact remains that, on balance, the new system is regarded as a success and a major improvement on the old arrangements. This bodes well for procedural reform elsewhere in the system and suggests lessons can be learned from the Sheriff Court experience.

The David Hume Institute is particularly happy to be able to publish these papers that both contribute to an important current public policy debate and extend the line of work that we started back in 1993. It is hoped that this is a theme to which we shall again return. As always, it is necessary to state that the Institute itself holds no collective view on these policy matters. Nevertheless, we feel that we can recommend the work of the authors produced here as worthwhile contributions to a policy debate of major importance.

Hector L MacQueen and Brian G M Main
Directors
The David Hume Institute

An Economic Perspective on the Costs of Justice

Brian G M Main

Introduction

At the outset, it is worthwhile to ask what we want from a system of civil justice. There are clear costs to be borne, both public and private: public in the running of the court system, and private in the paying of lawyers' fees and other related items. The private costs need not only be pecuniary, as there is often a substantial amount of delay in the legal process. The benefits, however, are huge. A well-run system of civil justice permits the enforcement of the property rights and contracts that allow a market economy to thrive, while also providing economic agents with the incentive to take an appropriate amount of care in their daily affairs lest they harm or injure others. Civil justice, therefore, promotes economic efficiency. Efficiency here implies that mutually beneficial contractual arrangements can be entered into, and that agents are induced to take the appropriate (welfare-maximising) decisions regarding care and precautions.

The Coase Theorem states that, in the absence of transaction costs, resource entitlements will be allocated efficiently in the market regardless of their initial allocation by law. This view brings into focus the importance of identified and enforceable property rights. It also underscores the desirability of low transaction costs – a consideration we return to in the discussion that follows, and one that poses something of a dilemma between accurate enforcement and low costs.

The civil justice system in Great Britain is currently undergoing a phase of self-examination and scrutiny. Recognition of dissatisfaction with the current operation of civil justice is most visible in the Woolf Report for England and Wales (1995,1996) and the Cullen Report (1995) for Scotland. There are clear signs that in both jurisdictions definite and marked procedural changes will follow from this process. Other commentators such as Cranston (1995), Murray (1997), Ogus (1997), Parratt (1997), Wadia (1997), and Zander (1995) examine the detailed proposals for reform that have emerged, but this paper takes a more general view and tries to identify the economic forces that must be confronted when considering a system of civil justice. Readers are also referred to a very useful survey of some of these issues by Rickman (1997).

2 THE REFORM OF CIVIL JUSTICE

We start from the position introduced above, namely that dispute resolution brings positive benefits to society. On the one hand, through the enforcement of agreements mutually beneficial exchanges and activities are encouraged. And, on the other hand, through the provision of redress harmful actions are discouraged. It then follows that finding ways to enhance the efficiency of existing dispute resolution mechanisms through the lowering of transaction costs will bring about gains in terms of the usual welfare measures. The discussion below centres on civil procedure in the court system, but it should be borne in mind that alongside the court system, indeed in its shadow, there is a range of less formal dispute resolution mechanisms at work. These include: alternative dispute resolution (ADR) mechanisms such as mediation and arbitration (e.g., by tribunals), the use of solicitors and other agents in reaching private orderings; and, most straightforward and undoubtedly most common, the completely informal resolution of disputes between private parties. All of these owe their effectiveness to the existence of that tribunal of last resort, namely the courts and the powers invested therein to hear cases, arrive at judgements, and to enforce rulings. Changes in the ways that courts function will also affect the operation of these alternative channels.

The key aspects of the court system that impact on transaction costs are the capacity of the system (in terms of volume of judicial services available), the procedures that are adopted in hearing grievances (inquisitorial versus adversarial, rules of evidence, discovery conventions, and so on), and any monopoly power granted to private sector agents through restricted rights of audience in the courts (advocates and solicitors). On the demand side, the extent to which costs are borne by the public sector (in the sense of court fees being below a level that allows the court administration to break even), or the extent to which private costs are subsidised by the state (through civil legal aid) will influence the decision to utilise the courts. With no market imperfections, and with state intervention only to organise and regulate the quality of judicial services, the system would expand to a level where the marginal costs of additional capacity equals the private marginal benefit to be gained by dispute resolution. There is a clear divergence between private decisions to use the courts and the public interest. These are discussed in detail by Shavell (1996), but the most obvious that will concern us here is the public good aspect whereby a court adjudication in one case allows many other disputes to settle with absolutely no recourse to the law.

At the moment, judicial capacity is administratively (some would say historically) determined, with civil capacity essentially being what is left after criminal case-demand has been serviced as a matter of priority (delay in criminal cases in Scotland is, of course, limited by statute to a maximum of 110 days for those in custody, and one year for those at liberty but charged). Low incomes and imperfect capital markets interact to produce a situation where concern regarding access to justice by the poor leads to some civil legal aid and/or contingency fee arrangement being found in most jurisdictions.

This paper[1] concentrates on the impact on the efficient disposal of civil justice of trials, procedural controls, fee shifting, fee design, and the failure of lawyers and the parties themselves to behave rationally. The discussion is set in a Scottish context, but for the most part the changing of defender to defendant, and pursuer to plaintiff puts the arguments into an England and Wales context.

We conclude that low-cost trials may not always be cheap if they involve a reduction in accuracy, i.e., in the ability of the court to establish the truth (wherever that is an appropriate concept). We also suggest that an imposed cap on legal expenditure can, in some instances, be mutually beneficial to the opposing parties involved in a dispute. There is also a discussion of procedural devices, such as payments into court, that can encourage out-of-court settlements in the range that the court itself would have decided. Finally, we demonstrate that lowering costs and/or increasing the efficiency of courts in reaching an accurate verdict need not lead to a reduction in court business, but may very well lead to a considerable expansion -some of which arises from reduced use of alternative and less formal channels, and some of which comes from a reduction in the volume of grievances that were hitherto not seen as worth pursuing. Subsidising any of these 'improvements' could only be justified after rather complex cost-benefit analysis that allowed for the direct and indirect changes in behaviour.

Trials

The business of the civil courts is dispute resolution, and recent analysis of the courts both by practitioners and by academics has tended to emphasise economic efficiency. One measure of an efficient court system is, ironically, the extent to which the courts are not used. Procedural arrangements such as disclosure, or the Scottish system of pleadings, can be seen as encouraging out-of-court settlements. Such settlements, although not the direct making of the judiciary, are, nevertheless, a product of the system. Trials as such may seem to be a minor part of the business of the law, but appearances are deceptive. What is going on elsewhere – in the unknown number of situations where no action is initiated, in the 90 to 95% of actions where settlement occurs before trial is 'bargaining in the shadow of the law' (Mnookin and Kornhauser (1979)) where the procedural rules laid down by the court play a key role in conditioning and influencing the negotiated out-of-court settlements between parties. Indeed, the shadow of the law extends to all negotiations, not just those that end up in the hands of lawyers.

There are two main ways in which to conduct trials: adversarial and inquisitorial. Tullock (1980) in the aptly named *Trials on Trial* argues for the efficiency of the latter. The reality is that the UK and most other Anglophone jurisdictions are firmly rooted in the adversarial approach. But whichever approach is utilised, it is important to recognise that the process of determining liability and assessing damages by trial is an imperfect process subject to error. Improving the accuracy of the court can bring gains, not only to those who have their day in court, but to all other individuals in society who have an interest in having a contract honoured, a damage repaired, or due care taken.

4 THE REFORM OF CIVIL JUSTICE

Assume a very simple representation of the decision to take a dispute to court as displayed in Figure 1, which is based on Tullock (1980). There are £X worth of damages at stake (not disputed). Assume further that the pursuer has a valid claim (i.e., the defender is in truth liable), but the proof of liability depends on the quality of evidence that can be presented to the court: the poorer the quality of evidence, the lower the probability of a verdict in favour of the pursuer (whom we assume to be in the right). Figure 1 assumes the quality of evidence varies from circumstance to circumstance, but taken over a large number of cases is distributed along AD, with any quality being equally likely in any particular case.

With the British system of cost allocation (loser pays) and with expected costs incurred by each side assumed to amount to one-third of the damages at stake, the probability of prevailing at trial must exceed 2 in 5 for the pursuer to find it worthwhile filing suit[2]. By similar logic the defender must see the probability of the pursuer winning to be less than 3 in 5 to bother defending the action (as opposed to settling out of court for agreed damages £X). From Figure 1 assuming that the solid line EFGD represents the probability of the court turning a certain quality of evidence into a verdict in favour of the pursuer (i.e., the court makes 'errors' in the sense that it cannot always on the basis of the evidence establish the true liability), then AB of disputes will settle without reference to law, BC cases will end up in court, and CD grievances will be ignored with impunity by the defender and go unanswered.

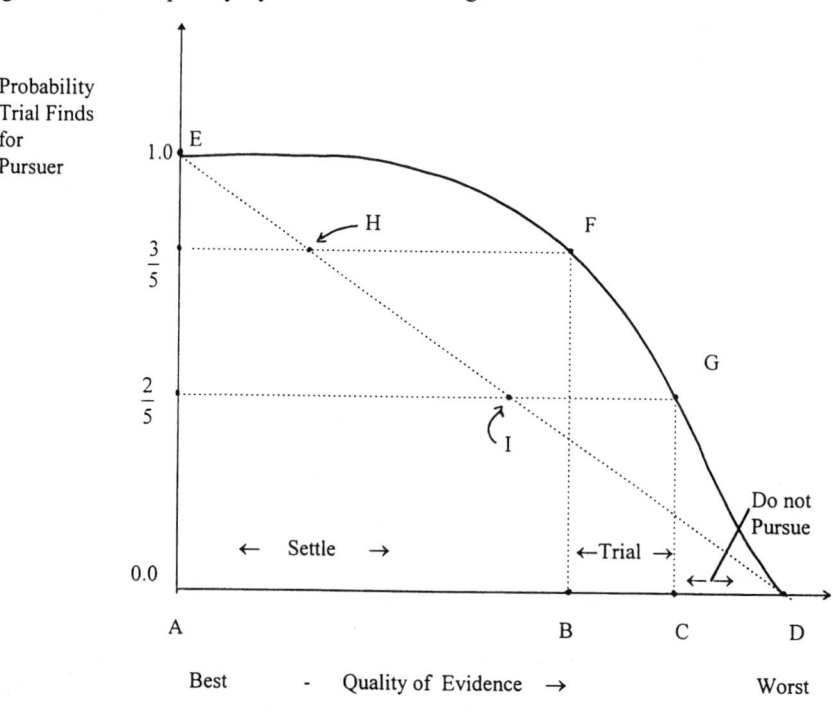

FIGURE 1   TRIAL AND SETTLEMENT

Thus AB cases benefit from the existence of the law without having to have recourse to it. The CD cases represent an inefficiency, as for those there is no incentive for the defender to take appropriate care, or one party will be inhibited from entering into an otherwise beneficial exchange. The impact of a deterioration in the efficiency of the courts can be seen by considering the dashed line EHID in Figure 1, as the transformation of evidence into a verdict for the pursuer becomes less likely for all qualities of evidence. Here the number of trials increases (between H and I), the number of grievances settled without reference to the law falls (to between E and H), and the number of grievances ignored rises (between I and D). All of this represents a decline in economic efficiency that may far outweigh any cost saving that was realised by allowing court standards to fall or procedures to be less rigorous.

Accuracy depends on both public spending (on subsidising courts, judges and other officials) and private spending (mainly court fees, expert witness fees, and lawyers' fees). The former is justified due to the public good aspect of civil justice, portrayed in Figure 1 as AB -those grievances that do not go to court but benefit from its existence. The latter is not entirely exogenous or predetermined, but decided by the litigants in conjunction with their lawyers. Now increased expenditure on one's legal representatives may allow better preparation of legal argument and more thorough consideration of the factual evidence. This in turn influences the chances of prevailing in court. It is, however, possible to claim that one disadvantage of the adversarial approach is its tendency to escalate expenditure on lawyers.

Such an outcome can be represented in game-theoretical terms as a prisoners' dilemma. This can be seen by reference to Figure 2 where the prisoners' dilemma nature of the situation is clear. Under the assumptions in Figure 2, if either party opts for a high-cost legal package while the other party chooses a low-cost package, then the net expected gains at trial are such as to make the high-cost package attractive[3]. Thus the pursuer sees a net expected gain of £13,500 rather than £8,000. Equivalently the defender sees expected losses reduced from £12,000 to £6,500 by switching to a high-cost regime. The problem is that when both parties chose a high-cost package the advantages are offsetting and both parties are left worse off than they would have been using a low-cost legal representation. But the prospect that the other side will opt to use high-cost legal representation leads both parties to do the same. In this sense the outcome is Pareto inferior – each party could be better off at no detriment to the other. But in the absence of some coercion or binding agreement neither party dare use the low cost form of legal representation. This lack of control of the other party's actions results in both opting for the Pareto inferior situation of high investment in legal costs, with corresponding expected outcomes of £6,000 and -£14,000 respectively. The situation is present in any fee-shifting regime but is exacerbated under the British rule. Plott (1987) has discussed this in terms of the 'dollar auction' problem with the British rule.

In addition to lawyers' fees, court fees can affect the dispensation of civil justice to the extent that higher court fees would find their way to provide enhanced judicial or courtroom capacity. In a recent *Hume Paper*, Gravelle (1996) argues that failing to charge realistic amounts for court time can lead

6 THE REFORM OF CIVIL JUSTICE

Assume:

Damages = £20,000

Costs to each party:

Low = £2,000
High = £4,000

Probability of Pursuer Winning:

		Defender's Costs	
		Low	High
Pursuer's	Low	0.50	0.25
Costs	High	0.75	0.50

Expected outcome: (Pursuer; Defender)

		Defender's Costs	
		Low	High
Pursuer's	Low	(£8,000; - £12,000)	(£500; - £6,500)
Costs	High	(£13,500; - £19,500)	(£6,000; - £14,000)

FIGURE 2   PRISONERS' DILEMMA OF LEGAL COSTS

to rationing by waiting. This is inefficient in the sense that the cost is borne by the litigants (as occurs with court charges), but there is no offsetting or matching gain to the supplier (unlike with charges). However reducing delay on its own will merely increase demand. Gravelle's conclusion is that pricing at marginal cost is best – i.e., charging users a realistic economic tariff for the use of the court system. This may suggest a move to increasing court charges and thereby increasing the provision of court time (judges). The impact of extra judicial resources is discussed further below.

In summary, trials have important public good attributes, although they can also lead to overspending on legal fees. Concepts of settlement and ADR are essentially meaningless in the absence of recourse to trial. What is done in court has a great impact not only on the handling of suits that do not come to court but also in the handling of the many more disputes that never reach the stage of assuming a formal grievance nature (bargaining in the shadow of the law). And, if trials are of essential importance, then so too is the procedural conduct of trials and the lead up to trials – standards of proof, statement of the complaint (pleadings in the Scottish system), discovery of evidence, permitted delays in hearings etc. We shall now turn to consider these details of procedure.

Procedure

As Zuckerman (1993) makes clear, views differ as to whether the effectivenessof procedural arrangements should be judged in the context of successful resolution of disputes or in the context of a search for an underlying truth. But all parties are agreed that impartiality is paramount. Equally, it is recognised that procedural arrangements designed to improve the seeking of truth are often open to abuse in the course of strategic bargaining.

Delay through procedural manipulation is a tactic that is thought to be used strategically to the benefit of both parties. Delay is often associated with the ability to run up legal costs either through access to own funds ('deep pockets') or through indemnity from costs through receipt of legal aid or trade union backing. In one empirical study of delay in the context of negligence suits filed against NHS Trusts in England, Fenn and Rickman (1997) identify low (i.e., subsidised) legal costs as an important causal factor. In this case it is the pursuer, using either legal aid or trade union funded legal representation, who is seen to drag things out. Legal expenses insurance does exist but is relatively poorly developed within the UK, although it is more popular in other European jurisdictions[4].

Of course, procedure is constantly evolving and periodically subjected to overhaul. A recent example of overhaul can be found in the amended procedures for defended ordinary actions in the Sheriff Courts in Scotland after January 1994. There, Morris and Headrick (1995) found that the old rules allowed frequent procedural diversions by way of sists, callings on the procedural roll, written motions, debates etc. In only a small minority (some 9%) of cases were none of these devices employed. In a study by KPMG Peat Marwick (1994) of the causes of delay in High Court and County Court cases in England the two key factors identified were the time taken in obtaining medical or other expert opinion and the inefficiency of solicitors in handling the cases. It was felt that active case management by the courts would not lead to a significant improvement.

In jurisdictions such as England and Wales and the USA, discovery, or seeking of documentary evidence from the opposing party, is a common source of delay (and of added costs). As Cooter and Rubinfeld (1994) make clear, discovery can increase accuracy, promote settlement and reduce transaction costs by lowering informational asymmetries. In practice, discovery forces the disclosure of disadvantageous facts – and this lowers false optimism by the other side and (as will be discussed below) will decrease trial probability. The increase in information will also align the terms of settlement nearer to those that would have been imposed by a court, and this may be more efficient. But a large part of the gain from discovery is redistributional (one side benefits to the cost of the other), and there is a case for preventing abuse of the discovery process by imposing costs – above a certain 'reasonable' level – on the requesting party.

An additional and substantive source of delay and costs is due to trial preparation. Hay (1995) recognises that uncertainty (and asymmetry) about exogenous information, such as the true extent of damages or the true nature of liability, may inhibit settlement in the early stages of dispute. But Hay argues further that the amount of case/ trial preparation invested by the opposing parties may present a further asymmetry of information that inhibits settlement in the later stages of the dispute, so making a trial more likely. Thus as the trial preparation proceeds each side's legal team becomes more and more familiar and expert in their own side of the case – possibly widening rather than narrowing each side's expectations regarding the trial outcome. Hay presents his arguments in game theoretic terms, but also acknowledges that other factors such as cognitive failure (over-estimating the strength of the case), strategic bargaining (preventing acceptance of a division of gains both parties know to exists in an attempt to secure a larger share), principal-agent problems (lawyers rejecting what a client would accept), and a preference for judicial resolution all represent other real causes of settlement failure. But if, as part of case management, there is a Woolf-type cap placed on costs (and hence trial preparation) this could lead to an improvement in efficiency, not only by inhibiting the mutual escalation of costs discussed earlier in this paper, but also by easing pre-trial settlement processes.

Of course, changing procedural rules can have both short-run and long-run effects on the number of trials. Any changes in procedure will initially introduce uncertainty and noise into the system – increasing the number of cases that go to trial. Things should thereafter settle down – but not necessarily to the same level of trials. This argument is demonstrated in Figure 3, due to Priest (1987), where in the top part of the diagram the standard of proof is set at q_0. Consequently, disputes with evidence in that range will go to trial. A change in the standard of evidence required (which can be thought of as a procedural change) will shift the evidentiary standard to q_1, say. In the transition phase one can expect a larger number of cases to go to trial as the exact position of q_1 is established among practitioners. Depending on the distribution of evidence in nature (among disputes arising) then, as in Figure 3, the new situation may well involve a higher number of disputes going to trial.

In a further discussion of procedure, Priest (1989) also questions the log-jam metaphor that gained popular currency in discussions of litigation delay during the 1960s and 1970s. Whereas it may be tempting to think of the legal system as cases (logs) floating into the trial system (a lake) and then flowing out of the system (on verdict or settlement), Priest points out that the situation is more complex. Simply increasing the number of logs (cases) leaving the system -by appointing more judges, say, or by simplifying procedure to reduce delay – will

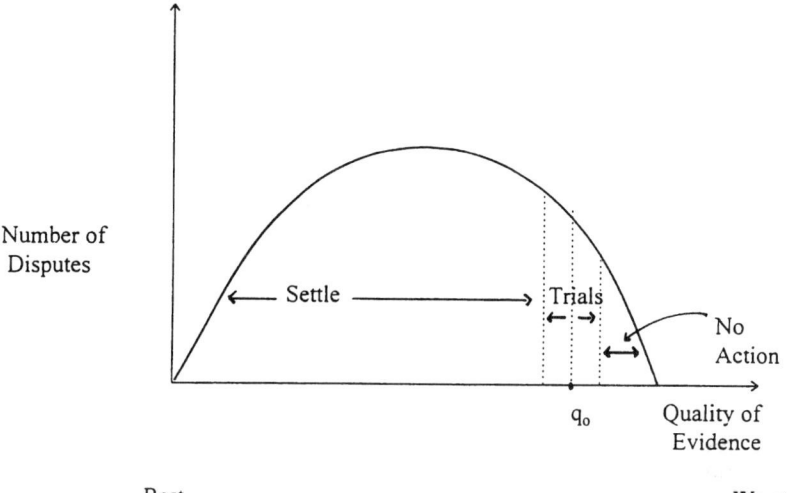

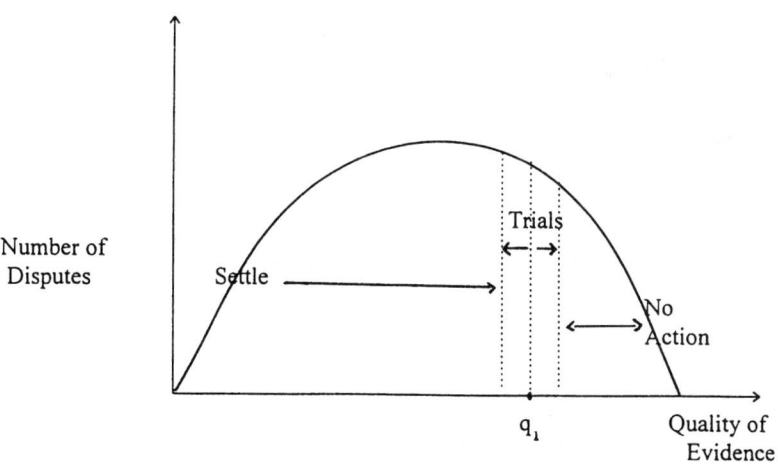

FIGURE 3 THE IMPACT OF CHANGING THE STANDARD OF PROOF

set off other changes that may counter the effect of the procedural innovations. This situation can best be captured in Posner's freeway metaphor. Thus, building an additional lane on the M25 will not necessarily reduce delays significantly. This is because motorists who had hitherto been using more minor roads, deterred by the prospect of delay on the M25, will switch onto the M25 and in so doing counteract at least some if not nearly all of the improvement in carrying capacity. The net result will be a much higher volume of traffic travelling at much the same speed as before. So too with the law courts and procedural delay. These points are discussed in a recent *Hume Paper* by Gravelle (1996).

Other procedural innovations such as the use of pre-trial conferences, alternative dispute resolution (ADR), modification of fee-shifting rules (e.g. Rule 68, discussed below) have long been used in the USA but not without critics. Owen Fiss (1985), in a famous essay against settlement, argues that there are in court cases important principles being clarified and developed and that while settlement may produce a private ordering the larger public good is overlooked – 'settlement is a poor substitute for judgement' (p1089). This elevated view of the business of the courts is challenged by those who see the overwhelming bulk of court business as being concerned with establishing the facts, which are most often not known or, at least, are in dispute, while the law applying to the dispute is generally accepted, albeit subject to a degree of manipulation for the sake of strategic advantage in negotiating a settlement.

Similarly, Shavell (1995) casts doubt on the need for public support of ADR. This is because *ex-ante* ADR procedural agreements between private parties will emerge where they are perceived to be of mutual benefit, and an ex-post imposition of ADR does not necessarily advance the interests of the parties. Given that by definition ADR was not taken into account by the parties as they entered their agreement, and that ex-post voluntary ADR must have going to court as a credible threat, then adding ADR to the process ex-post does not change behaviour in any cost-reducing way. When ADR is of a binding nature then, as a cheaper alternative, it will be used when ADR perfectly predicts the outcome of the trial, although it may also deter early settlement. When prediction is less than perfect then trial may be less frequent, not only because ADR is cheaper but because the parties' views on the outcome of ADR may diverge more than their views about trial, thereby making ADR a 'better bet'.

It seems clear then that procedural innovations (cost-capping, case management, charging for discovery, introducing information technology, training solicitors in negotiation etc.) can have a beneficial impact on the cost of individual litigation, both in pecuniary and in time costs. But the overall impact may be to increase the volume of suits filed, albeit with many of these suits settling or being dropped before trial. The net social benefit is unclear and it is an issue to which we shall return blow when we discuss fee design. First, however, it is necessary to consider the impact of fee-shifting regimes on the proclivity to file suit, to settle, and to affect the level of final outcome.

Fee shifting

One major consideration when evaluating the efficiency of court procedures in effecting grievance settlements is the fee-shifting rules that are in place (i.e., who pays the court costs and the legal fees of the parties involved). There is a well-rehearsed debate between the virtues of the American rule (parties pay own costs) and the British rule (loser pays) which has recently been extensively reviewed by Katz (1997) and in a recent special issue of the *Chicago-Kent Law Review* (1995). In truth the practice in the USA and in Europe varies substantially in the detail of implementation from the stereotypical view, as Pfenningstorf (1984) makes clear. There are over 150 state and federal statutes in the USA that allow an element of cost shifting (e.g., California State Rule 998 or Rule 68 in the US Federal Courts), mainly in recognition of 'offers to compromise' whereby the defendant has made a pre-trial offer to settle that turns out, in the light of the trial, to have been reasonably generous. Federal and state courts also have the power to indemnify individuals against egregious abuse of process.

Equally, the interpretation of the loser-pays rule is far from being harmonised in its implementation across Europe. In the UK, one of the practical departures from the stereotypical view of the British rule is the ability of the defender to make what is variously known as 'offers into court' or 'payments into court'. This is an offer-based rule of cost allocation similar to that found in the USA. Under such a procedural rule, if the offer made by the defender is refused and yet is not bettered by any subsequent court award then the pursuer is liable for the 'taxed' (officially verified and scrutinised) expenses of the defender that arise after the date of the offer. As Hurst (1995) makes clear, such taxed ('*inter-partes*' basis) costs are likely to be less than the full costs ('solicitor and client' basis), but there remains a considerable incentive to settle as costs rise significantly once the courtroom stage is reached. The general idea is, of course, that this cost-shifting rule will encourage the parties to move towards a settlement. This arrangement of offers to compromise, echoed in Rule 68 in the US Federal Courts, in California State Rule 998, and in many other similar state statutes across the USA, is not without its critics who generally view it as a pro-defender device. The empirical impact of the arrangement in the USA is frequently substantially weakened in practice by restricting the scope of costs to cover only court costs, thus excluding attorney fees.

In an attempt to further expedite out-of-court or early settlement, both Woolf (1995, 1996) and Cullen (1995) have proposed that the right to make offers into court be extended to the pursuer. This is a slightly more complex arrangement, as in order for the court to be bettering (more generous than) the pursuer's offer to settle, then the defender must have been found liable and hence, under the loser-pays rule, is already responsible for the pursuer's costs. Lord Woolf (1996: 112) regards the offer to settle as 'capable of making an important contribution to the change of culture which is fundamental to the reform of civil justice'. Thus, to create an incentive for the defender in such circumstances, Woolf suggests a punitive level of interest rate (from 5 to 25 percentage points above the conventional prevailing rate) on the awarded damages with the interest due to be calculated from the date of the offer into court.

Cullen (1995: 59) underscores similar proposals under consideration by the Court of Session Rules Council that 'the defender should normally be found liable in expenses at an increased level where the pursuer has succeeded in "beating his own offer" '. Under procedures which were briefly tested with effect from 23 September 1996 in the Court of Session (S.I. 1996/2168(S.175)), offers into court by the pursuer subsequently matched or beaten by the Court's award would have resulted in double costs being charged. Prospective complications in implementation that would have arisen in cases where there were multiple defenders forced the rule change to be rescinded after some seven weeks, with effect from 14 November 1996 (S.I. 1996/2769). Tiplady (1991) suggests that extending to the pursuer reimbursement of costs on a liability basis (i.e., on the full solicitor and client basis) rather that on a taxed (*inter-partes*) basis would provide incentive enough.

The original approach to the question of pre-trial negotiation is due to Landes (1971), Posner (1973) and Gould (1973). These authors concentrate on the bargaining range (the difference between the likely gain to the pursuer if s/he goes to court and the likely out-of-pocket expense to the defender). They assume that trial expenditures and the probability of prevailing at trial are invariant to the cost-shifting regime in place. The essential view here is that much as it takes a difference of opinion to make a horse race, then it is the difference in perceived probabilities of court outcomes that leads the opposing parties to court. No attempt is made in this literature to determine unique settlement values. The focus of analysis is rather the settlement range and the consequent probability of a suit being brought or of a suit, once brought, going to trial. The notion being that with a wide bargaining range an out-of-court settlement is more likely.

Figure 4 illustrates the Posner/Landes/Gould approach in terms of the American rule for costs. The pursuer anticipates a probability of prevailing at trial of P_p and an awarded damages level of D_p, resulting in an expected trial outcome of $T_p = P_p D_p$. With a similar notation for the defender, it is clear that there is scope for settlement if $T_p < T_d$. This situation is often thought of in terms of the parties having similar views about the damages involved but being relatively 'pessimistic' in the sense that P_p P_d. Here P_d refers to the defender's estimate of the pursuer's chance of winning in court. Equivalently, if the parties are relatively 'optimistic' then P_p P_d, both expect to do better at trial, and trial is likely. The presence of litigation costs widens the gap between the parties' expectations and hence the scope for a mutually advantageous out-of-court settlement. Out-of-court settlement produces a surplus that can be shared to mutual advantage between the protagonists. Of course settlement itself is not free from costs, but on the assumption that settlement costs, C_{sp}, are less than trial costs, C_{tp}, then the zone of possible agreement (ZoPA) is widened.

Such has been the success of this approach that it has come to be known as 'the LPG model'. The paper by Shavell (1982) marks its high point. That paper suggests that the British rule will lower the number of suits and the number of trials if the probability of pursuer success is relatively low. On the other hand, the number of suits and possibly also of trials under the British rule will rise if the probability of success is relatively high. The approach has received some empirical support, e.g., Hughes and Snyder (1995), and continues to have its adherents.

AN ECONOMIC PERSPECTIVE ON THE COSTS OF JUSTICE

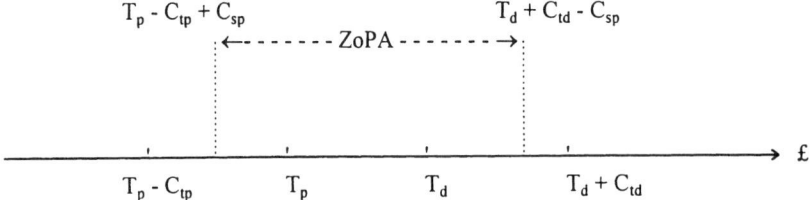

where,

T_p = Pursuer's expected award at trial

= $P_p \cdot D_p$

i.e., Pursuer's estimate of probability of winning (P_p) times expected damages (D_p)

T_d = Defender's expected loss at trial

= $P_d D_d$

i.e., Defender's estimate of probability of pursuer winning (P_d) times expected damages (D_d)

C_{tp} = Expected trial cost to pursuer
C_{td} = Expected trial cost to defender
C_{sp} = Expected (out of court) settlement transaction costs to pursuer
C_{sd} = Expected settlement transaction costs to defender
ZoPA = Zone of possible agreement

Assumes relative pessimism, $T_p < T_d$

FIGURE 4 THE BARGAINING RANGE

But nothing in the LPG approach allows for strategic behaviour in the sense of litigants choosing levels of expenditure on lawyers or in choosing negotiating offers based either on privately held information (e.g., truth about liability or extent of damages) and/or as part of a calculated strategy to secure the lion's share of the available surplus arising from an out-of-court settlement. In this vein, Cooter, Marks and Mnookin (1982) point out that there are reasons other than the excessive optimism of the opposing parties that land them in expensive court procedure – the distributional problem compounded by strategic behaviour in bargaining can also lead to the relatively inefficient outcome of a court appearance. Most theoretical analysis has concentrated on the asymmetry of information between the two parties. Either there is uncertainty regarding the level of damage suffered by the pursuer, as in Reinganum and Wilde (1986), or there is uncertainty regarding the degree of liability to be attached to the defender, as in Bebchuk (1984) and P'ng (1987).

These strategic bargaining papers allow a one-shot type of bargaining (a take-it-or-leave-it approach). Spier (1992), on the other hand, specifically focuses on the dynamics of pre-trial negotiation. Allowing defenders to have private knowledge about the trial she finds that settlements occur with a relatively high probability in the early stages of negotiation but that this probability of settlement falls off as negotiations continue. However, the rate of settlement recovers markedly as the date of the trial approaches. This theoretical finding is, of course, consistent with the widely recognised proclivity for cases to settle 'at the door of the court'.

In the literature, most analysis of the impact of 'offers into court' has been couched in terms of the most widely known US rule of this type, namely Federal Rule 68, adopted in 1938. Miller (1986) concludes that this arrangement does indeed encourage settlements, although he suggests that the rule's most significant effect is to redistribute wealth from the pursuer to the defender by increasing the bargaining power of the defender. Spier (1994) is more definite if still equivocal, finding that where there is asymmetry of information regarding the level of damages then Rule 68 increases settlements, but where the asymmetry pertains to the probability of prevailing at trial then Rule 68 decreases the probability of settlement.

The conclusions that can be drawn from the theoretical work in this area are therefore of a highly qualified nature. But whereas one would usually look to empirical work for more definitive guidance or for a resolution of theoretical ambiguities, there has been remarkably little work of that kind in this field. This is due to the difficulty in generating any data in an area where confidentiality is the rule. Only a small proportion of cases (around 5%) go to trial ('proof' in Scotland). For the 95% or so that settle out of court, albeit possibly settling after a long time in the court system, little or nothing is known about the level of damages agreed or the costs charged, unless the latter become a matter of dispute between the parties. Of those decided by the court (almost always a judge in civil matters) the level of costs will be the subject to 'taxation' in a court-related assessment procedure (see Hurst (1995)), but even here agreement between the parties on costs can void this step, and once again the data are not to be found in the public domain. The desire for secrecy on these matters is driven by concern for reputation and a perceived need on the part of the defenders to strengthen subsequent bargaining power against later pursuers. Finally, jurisdictional differences are so marked that the usual type of comparative work is fraught with difficulty.

Exceptions to this lack of empirical work can be found in Snyder and Hughes (1990) and Hughes and Snyder (1995). They have been able to utilise data based on a natural experiment when the State of Florida switched from the American rule to the British rule for malpractice litigation between July 1980 and September 1985. These authors conclude that the British rule encourages litigation, although leading to more claims to be dropped and more settlements to occur as the claim moves to trial. Of those suits reaching court the outcomes are subsequently more pro-plaintiff in terms of decisions on liability and size of damages, this suggesting a sorting mechanism. Thus, as the case proceeds and information is obtained and clarified, the parties revise their prior probabilities of succeeding in court. The prospect of bearing the other party's costs in the event of a defeat in court causes weaker cases to be withdrawn or settled. In the Hughes and Snyder investigation in Florida, this seemed to leave plaintiffs who reached the court with relatively strong cases.

While fee shifting plays an obviously important part in determining the use of court time, attention recently has focused more on the level of costs rather than the distribution of costs. There is a widespread normative view that unlike most other goods access to justice is a merit good and that near universal access to justice is somehow an important part of civil society. This is expressed in section 2.9 of the Report of the Hughes Commission (quoted in Goriely(1995)) whose view of the need for legal services was:

> – firstly enabling the client to identify, and if he judges it appropriate, to choose a legal solution; and, secondly, enabling the client to pursue a chosen legal solution.

But since the first moves in 1945 to provide civil legal aid, there has been steady and recently almost exponential growth in the costs of the scheme. Nominally the Legal Aid Board polices the scheme, but solicitors are effectively in the driving seat – creating the usual sort of supplier-induced demand problems that are discussed in some detail in recent *Hume Papers* by Bowles (1996) and by Gray, Fenn and Rickman (1996). The USA's Legal Services Corporation was always strictly cash limited. Canada and Australia now have cash limited schemes, and recent reforms in England and Wales will produce similar effects.

In summary, it appears as if fee-shifting rules do effect the likelihood of settlement versus trial. They also impact on the level of legal costs incurred – sometimes to an inefficient extent. The Woolf proposals (echoed in Cullen) regarding capping of costs within the multi-track designation of the case can be viewed as an attempt to avoid this inefficient outcome. The extension of offers into court to the pursuer can also be argued to promote more out-of-court settlement. Mechanisms to reduce the cost of civil legal aid or to make existing legal aid expenditures go further include establishing cash-limited 'franchises' with responsibility for providing civil legal aid in defined geographic areas. More sweeping and more general recommendations for reform are aimed at reducing the overall costs of legal services by attacking what is seen to be the monopoly power of the legal profession. Some of these aspects are reviewed in Stephen and Love (1997). Progress in reducing this monopoly power has been made over recent decades: the abolition of mandatory fee schedules or scale fees; permitting advertising; extending the right of representation, e.g., to a new hybrid of solicitor-advocate in Scotland; and eroding

16 THE REFORM OF CIVIL JUSTICE

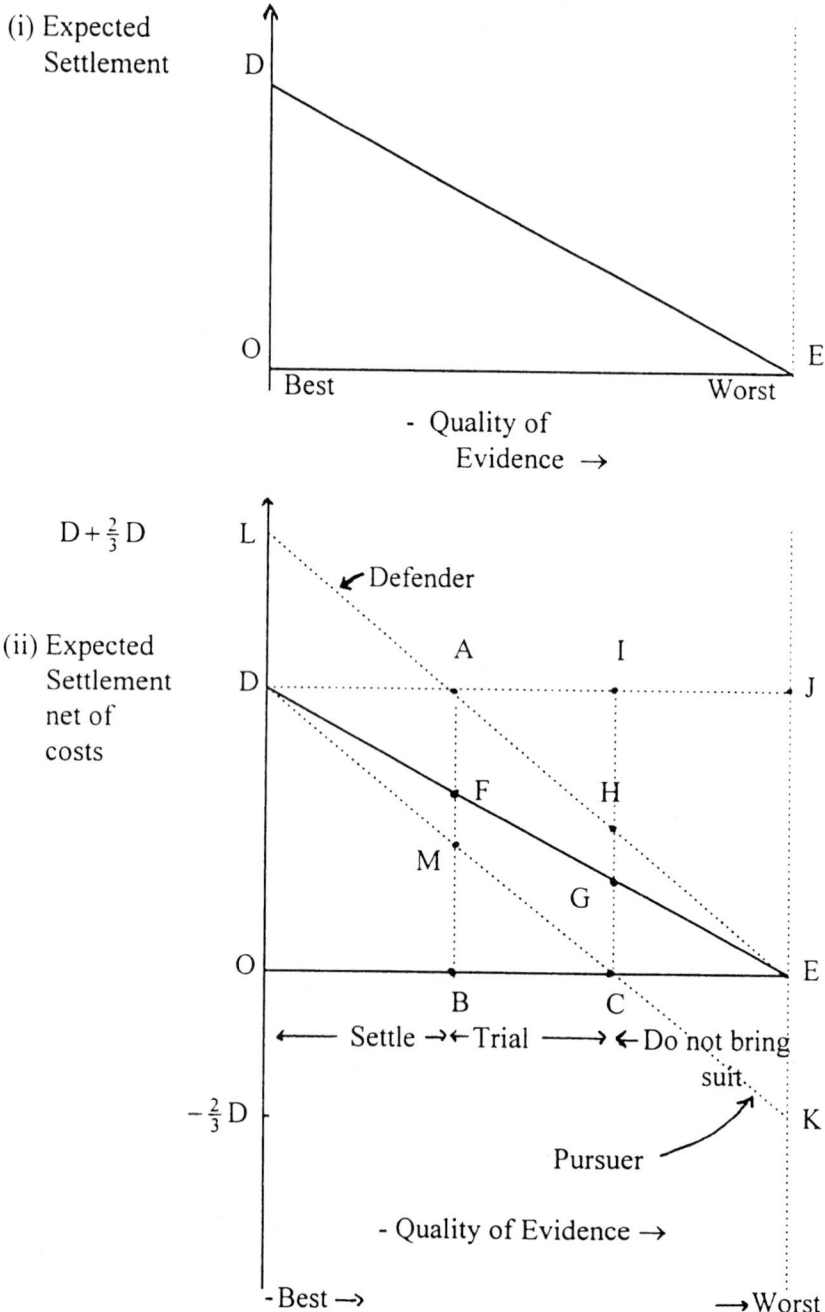

FIGURE 5 SUIT, TRIAL, SETTLEMENT

exclusive rights, e.g., on conveyancing in England and Wales. But many issues remain unresolved such as restrictions on organisational form, entry restrictions, and restrictions on fee contracts. Aspects of fees that remain to be discussed are the level of fees and the structure of fees. It is to these topics that we now turn.

Fee level and fee design

The impact of fee structures in determining which cases go to court and which do not, has ramifications far beyond the courtroom. This can be demonstrated by means of a simple diagram adapted from Tullock (1980) and similar to Figure 1. In Figure 5 it is assumed that grievances (all assumed to be valid on the pursuer's side) arise with a varying quality of evidence. For any given standard of evidence and rules of court procedure we shall assume that there is a well known probability of the pursuer's claim (for fixed damages D) being upheld in court. This leads to an expected trial outcome (probability of judgement times the level of damages) as a function of the quality of the evidence. Assume this is shown by DE in Figure 5(i). Assume further that the structure of fees is that each party will spend one-third of the level of the claim on legal fees and that the British cost-shifting rule (loser pays) is applied. Thus the pursuer's expected net outcome after trial varies from a gain of D to a loss of 2D/3 depending on the quality of the evidence (along DCK in Figure 5(ii)). The defender's expected outcome after trial varies in a similar way from a loss of (D + 2D/3) in the face of good evidence and the consequent loss of the case with all costs to pay, to zero in the face of little or no evidence (along LAE in Figure 5(ii)).

Figure 5(ii) reveals that the defender can always limit losses by settling for D and does so for OB cases, which never enter the court system – these are efficiently resolved. In addition the combination of fee structure and standard of proof implies that the expected net gain of the pursuer will fall below zero for CE cases which will, consequently, never enter the court system. For BC cases, however, trial will proceed. Total legal costs are given by area AHCM.

Figure 6 reproduces the situation represented in Figure 5 except that we have assumed a higher standard of accuracy by the courts. For a given standard of evidence there is now a higher probability that the court will (correctly) find for the pursuer. The line DE is, for example, higher for all levels of evidence. The pursuer can expect to get nearer to the true level of damages (having more chance of successfully proving the liability of the defender) than was previously the case – for all levels of evidence. After allowing for fees, the pursuer's expectations shift to DC'K and the defender's to LA'E. Compared with the previous standard of accuracy (in Figure 5 and reproduced in the dashed lines in Figure 6), the number of just grievances being ignored falls from CE to C'E cases. In addition the number of grievances that are settled without recourse to law rises from OB to OB'. Both of these moves represent increases in efficiency. Finally the number of cases going to court changes for BC to B'C' which may or may nor represent a fall.

18 THE REFORM OF CIVIL JUSTICE

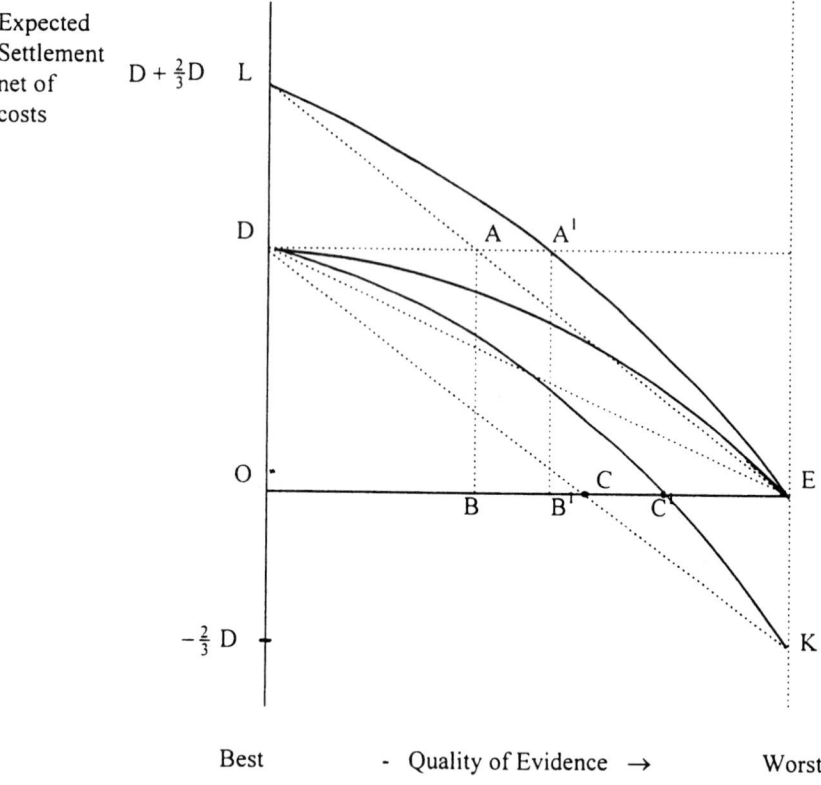

FIGURE 6   THE IMPACT OF ACCURACY IN THE COURT

Kaplow and Shavell (1996) argue that, as long as judgements are on average correct and assess the expected damages (to make whole), then further refinements to match exactly the damage done to particular pursuers may not be economically efficient if the tortfeasor cannot *ex ante* anticipate the exact amount of damage that will be caused but only the average outcome (e.g. car crash). But this is a different type of accuracy from that under discussion here.

The same diagrammatic representation can be used to demonstrate the impact of lower costs. Reverting the standard of accuracy in Figure 5 but reducing costs so that each party expends only one-sixth of the damages level, D, then it can be seen in Figure 7 that the cost-benefit calculus for each side changes. Because of the lower costs (represented by the dotted line in Figure 7), now only cases to the left of A* (i.e., OB*) settle out of court. On the other hand, only those to the right of C* (i.e., C*E) have such poor evidentiary support as not to be worth pursuing through the legal system. This represents an increase in economic efficiency as now there is more likelihood both of the appropriate amount of care and attention being taken, and also of mutually beneficial agreements being made. On the other hand a far higher number of grievances end up in court. The number of cases which the defender was

AN ECONOMIC PERSPECTIVE ON THE COSTS OF JUSTICE   19

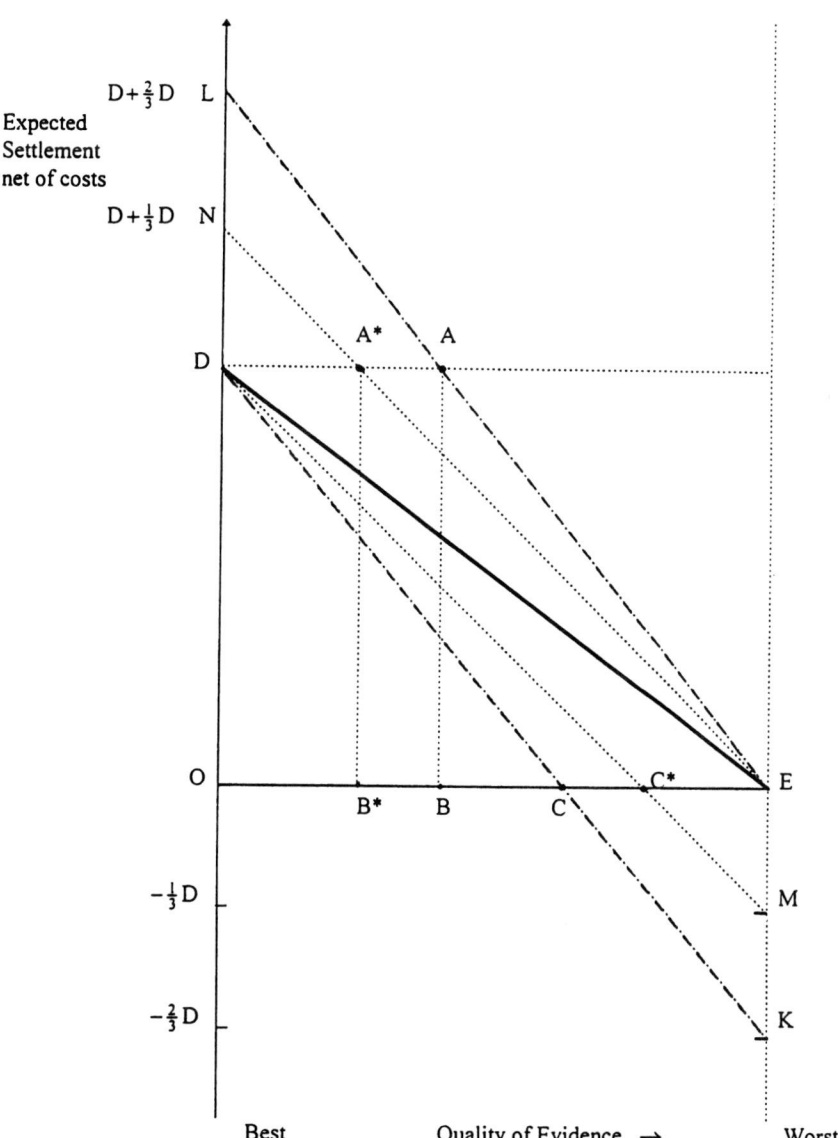

FIGURE 7   THE IMPACT OF LOWER LEGAL COSTS

previously happy to settle without reference to the court falls from OB to OB*, and the number of grievances in court rises to B*C* from BC. In delivering this increase in equity (more grievances receive some sort of redress) and efficiency (e.g., the tortfeasor is held accountable for more of the grievances), there has been a considerable increase in court business. In addition, we have assumed a constant standard of accuracy in Figure 7. But as Figure 6 shows, if there is any concomitant reduction in accuracy as costs fall then the net benefit is unclear. The net impact on overall wealth creation and economic well-being is unclear. Increased access to justice has brought gains, but possibly at a cost.

In addition to reducing fees (and hence transaction costs), the structure of fees can affect outcomes. Gravelle and Waterson (1993) provide a discussion in the British context. There are essentially three ways in which fees may be structured. The first is the hourly rate and is used in all jurisdictions. Due to the principal-agent problem of the client being dependent on the lawyer when it comes to judging the appropriate amount of legal services to put into a case, this can lead to biases. The lawyer is in a position to work on (rewarded at an hourly rate) well past the stage where the incremental value to the case falls below the additional costs incurred (even after factoring out an allowance for the increased probability of victory and hence cost avoidance under the British system – and the Tax Master will not necessarily allow all costs even in the eventuality of victory, generally ruling on a more narrow '*inter-partes*' rather than a 'solicitor and client' basis).

On the other hand with a contingency fee, the second type of fee arrangement whereby the lawyer secures a proportion of any award if successful and zero compensation if unsuccessful, there is an incentive to settle too soon. As only part-beneficiary to the final award, the lawyer will settle the case when her/his share of the expected increase in settlement falls below the extra cost of an hour's input. Settlement just before the major investment of a court trial is taken by many to be a characteristic of this feeing arrangement. In contrast, the client, facing a marginal cost of lawyer effort equal to zero under the contingent fee arrangement, would press the lawyer to invest ever more hours of effort. Apart from this potential conflict of interests, the lawyer is usually in control and one can therefore expect an under-investment of effort. By contrast, Rickman (1996) and others have predicted that the contingency fee arrangement may add sufficient credibility to the lawyer in negotiating (through "hard bargaining") that the resultant settlement is significantly higher. There is one further advantage to the contingency fee arrangements in that they permit the experienced and/or diversified lawyer to take on risks that would be unattractive to an individual pursuer. This allows those for whom the financing of a legal action is a problem (the poor and the risk averse) to have their case promoted, albeit at the sacrifice of some of the potential damages. The contingency fee can also be tapered to rise (or fall) as a percentage of the recovery or as a function of the stage of settlement.

The use of any contingent fee arrangements in England and Wales, in Canada, and other jurisdictions has been restricted out of concern regarding 'maintenance' or 'champerty', whereby lawyers assume an interest in the outcome of the trial. Halpern and Turnbull (1982) provide some further discussion. There has been some relaxation in England and Wales with a removal of the statutes prohibiting champerty and, more recently, a condoning of conditional fees. Under this arrangement, the lawyer will receive double (or some other agreed multiple) the taxable fee if the case is successful but zero otherwise. This conditional fee is akin to the speculative fee that has been available in Scotland for many years, and forms the third class of fee arrangement that is possible. This situation is closer to that of an hourly rate than of contingency – at the margin the reward for an extra hour's effort is (double, say) the hourly rate discounted by the probability of success which is only being marginally affected by that last hour of effort. It does, however, represent a shift of the risk of failure onto the lawyer and away from the client or legal-aid board. There is the added complication that under the loser-pays system of allocating costs there is a need to find insurance against that contingency. If this is difficult to obtain or expensive then some of the poorest litigants may be disuaded from pursuing their grievance. The proposal that all legal-aid cases in England and Wales move to such an arrangement and away from the traditional paid-by-the-clock system has, for this and other reasons, provoked substantial resistance.

Some commentators, e.g., Hay (1997), have suggested that an optimal fee structure would leave the lawyer a large fraction of the recovery in the event of a trial but only a small fraction if the case settles. Many other variants are possible. As mentioned above, Scotland has long permitted the adoption of cases on a speculative basis (a multiple of the hourly rate if successful, but no fee if the case fails). It may be that the recent move in England and Wales to introduce a similar practice in legal-aid cases will encourage further change in this area in the UK in the near future.

Lawyers' and parties' behaviour

Mnookin and Kornhauser (1979) provide a discussion of the aspects of legal representation that can result in grievances going to trial. The most obvious is as the outcome of strategic behaviour that has backfired – where at least one party is obdurately but knowingly holding out for a larger share of the gains from settlement than is truly necessary to settle the case. Secondly there are transaction costs which when high may lead the parties to settle, or indeed to simply ignore the grievance (these are demonstrated in the variations of Tullock's diagrams in Figures 5 to 7 above). Thirdly there is the matter of the bargaining endowment that is created by the existing legal and procedural rules. These can include discovery, fee shifting, offers into court etc., which have been discussed above. Fourthly, there is the degree of uncertainty concerning the legal outcome if the matter were to be resolved in court. This encourages the risk averse to settle – often the pursuer who may be a one-time player as against the defender who may be a repeat player with a reputation to consider and the possibility of spreading risk over many cases. Most of these points have already been discussed above, but there are some additional aspects of the client-lawyer relationship that should be mentioned.

In a recent *Hume Paper* on the subject of access to justice, several authors argue that the relationship between the client and lawyer fails to bring about an efficient delivery of legal services due to the highly imperfect market for lawyers' services. The market is seen to be imperfect because of asymmetry of information between lawyer and client (the lawyer knowing much more about

22 THE REFORM OF CIVIL JUSTICE

how the system works), restrictions on the types of contract allowed (prohibitions on full contingency fees for example), and restrictive practices arising from the operation of various agencies such as the Law Societies, the Faculty of Advocates, the Bar Council etc. This is a strong argument. In an additional contribution to the debate, Ogus (1997) emphasises the limited prospects for effective reform as long as the legal profession enjoys its quasi-monopoly and self-regulatory status. Ogus argues that procedural rules are essentially established by the suppliers, that there exists a prisoner's dilemma aspect that drives up costs, and that principal-agent considerations in terms of the ways in which lawyers are remunerated lead to excessive costs. While judicial management holds out promise of improved efficiency, its effectiveness depends on the tastes and incentives of judges. If one accepts that the current rules are inadequately enforced, then this holds out little hope for any new rules.

There are also some less structural and more behavioural considerations that merit our consideration. These behavioural considerations are essentially social-psychological in nature and are reviewed by Korobkin and Guthrie (1997). Some clients are simply not interested in settlement, wishing at all costs to 'have their day in court' or to establish a precedent. These are to some extent consumption aspects of litigation. Settlement decisions are also conditioned by the social context of the situation. Various cognitive biases (errors or breakdowns in rationality) can arise due to anchoring or framing of negotiations, or by escalating commitment – often exacerbated by a need to reduce cognitive dissonance (subconscious face saving), and a host of other factors. Anchoring of negotiations can occur due to one side or other becoming overly attached to an opening offer/demand, to the level of an award made in some other salient case, to the amount that is needed for some purpose but has no bearing on the case at hand, and so on. Similarly, framing can distort decision-making through the context in which the demand or offer is made. Thus, otherwise acceptable offers to settle may prove unattractive if they are allowed to be presented as a reduction from some opening demand rather than an improvement on the original position (zero). Escalating commitment arises when early concessions in the negotiation dance are allowed to accelerate the level of expected concessions from the other side rather than leading to a convergence.

All of these are human failings in decision-making, and while training can alert people to be watchful for such tendencies, they are difficult to eradicate from the system in any fundamental way. They do represent sound reasons for employing trained representatives or agents (lawyers in this context) to handle the negotiation. Empirical work conducted by Kritzer (1991) and by Genn (1987) emphasises the very human and person-specific effects that arise in reaching settlements. Genn's phrase 'hard bargaining' has entered the lexicon of legal terms.

Summary and Conclusion

Society has a strong interest in the quality of its civil justice system. If economic welfare is to be maximised then it is necessary that as many mutually beneficial contracts be entered into as possible. It is also necessary that agents take an appropriate level of care against harming others in the course of their daily business. For these and other reasons, an effective civil justice system promotes economic well-being by providing a binding arbiter of disputes. The court system has an influence well beyond those grievances that reach the court room, or those that reach the stage of filing suit. An accurate and affordable system of civil justice increases the efficiency of all transactions and is a clear priority for any society.

By changing procedures, by adjusting the level and structure of legal fees, by augmenting the judicial capacity of the court system, by subsidising legal costs, by charging market responsive for court time, by imposing judicial case management, and so on, it is possible to have a direct impact on the dispensation of civil justice. But at the end of the day, the overall impact of any such changes will depend on a complex set of interactions among the various players in the game (parties, lawyers, judges) and may differ markedly from that first intended.

There are many ways in which the current civil judicial system can be improved. Enhancing the capacity of the system by increasing the volume of judicial services available (that product of court rooms and judges sitting in them) would reduce the amount of delay involved in court procedure. Increased throughput could also be achieved by empowering judges to move from being impartial referees to acting more as informed, disinterested insiders by providing them with a more interventionist case-management role. Here, however, one has to worry about accuracy, as we have seen above that the efficiency of the court in determining the 'truth' can affect the decision of whether to bring a suit, or whether to settle a suit that has been raised, or whether to reach a private accommodation, or whether to just not bother complaining at all.

Capacity and efficiency can also be improved by deregulating the solicitors and advocates who represent individuals in court. In particular, the ability of the client and the lawyer to reach private and mutually advantageous contract regarding the fees and the manner of disposition of the case should be encouraged. To this end, further deregulation of advertising, unrestricted rights of audience, competition on fee level, and ability to agree fee design (contingent, hourly rate etc.) would all represent improvements. There is also substantial scope for introducing market-determined court fees as a way of adjusting judicial capacity in the system. Significant progress has been made on some of these dimensions over the last two decades, but there remains some way to go.

Some technical aspects regarding court procedure also merit consideration. These include the extension to the pursuer of the right to make an offer to settle, the ability to limit the strategic use of the discovery process, and the possibility of capping exposure to own and other party's costs.

The scope for improving economic efficiency seems reasonably clear, but there are some unavoidable distributional questions. As has been spelled out above, an increased efficiency in the system is almost certain to be accompanied by an increased utilisation. Part of this increase will involve cases which would have settled privately or through some alternative dispute resolution mechanism. The outcomes here are likely to be little different from those that occurred in the shadow of the law – save that there will be some additional potential gains available owing to the increased efficiency of the courts. Another part of the increase, however, will involve grievances that were hitherto ignored owing to the high costs of seeking remedy. These cases will now be addressed and the pursuer (the damaged party) is likely to gain – both by being 'made whole' in the event of damage, and by being able to engage in a productive activity in the assurance that redress is possible if things go wrong. The defender (i.e., tortfeasor in certain classes of case, or party in breach in others) is certain to be worse off. But as we are reducing harm, this situation does not carry the usual normative overtones that arise when welfare criteria of the Hicks/ Kaldor variety are applied.

The remaining distributional question is a more thorny one. With the likely increased scope of business for the courts, there will be a class of potential clients who because of a combination of low income and imperfect capital markets are excluded from pursuing what would otherwise be a viable suit. Civil legal aid is the usual remedy. But these funds are already under pressure and subject to stringent means-testing. It is possible, of course, that some of the increase in efficiency comes about through lower priced legal services (solicitors' and advocates' fees, for example). It is, therefore, possible that even in the face of increased demand the civil legal aid bill might fall. But this depends on a relatively inelastic demand for legal services and a relatively large efficiency-induced shift in the supply curve for those services. Empirically this presents a rather imponderable question at this time. But one thing is certain, and that is without downward pressure on legal costs an increase in the capacity of judicial services and the consequent reduction in delay will drive demand for civil legal aid upwards.

In conclusion, there seem to be a range of policy options for the government to consider. One, the status quo, is relatively safe, although it leaves us in a situation recognised by Woolf, Cullen and other commentators as unsatisfactory. A second option is to undertake a radical transformation of the court system, imposing charges that in turn facilitate expansion of judicial capacity while at the same time introducing reforms in procedure (case-management, offers into court, caps on fees etc.) and reforms in the legal profession (encouraging more competition in terms of representation, advertising, fee negotiation etc.) that place downward pressure on the cost of taking a case to court. This could vastly increase the capacity of the most formal dispute resolution mechanism channel in the country while leaving civil legal aid budget not too greatly increased. Other policy options lying between these first two – particularly the expansion of court capacity – threaten to have disturbing distributional effects, although their efficiency gains would remain.

Notes

1. Thanks are due to Hector MacQueen and Alan Peacock for helpful discussions and comments during the preparation of this paper. Remaining errors are my own.

2. Assuming: £X is the level of damages involved (not disputed); £X/3 is the level of costs incurred by both sides if the matter goes to court; P is the probability that on the evidence to hand the court will find for the pursuer. Then, to the pursuer, the expected gain from trial (assuming a loser pays allocation rule for costs) is:

   PX − (1−P)2X/3

   this being the balance of the expected gains if successful and the expected costs if the case fails (loser pays).

   To the defender, the expected cost of trial is:

   PX + P2X/3

   this being the expected cost of being found liable. There is no cost to the defender if not found guilty.

   For the pursuer the expected gains must be greater than zero to make trial worth while, i.e., $P > 2/5$. For the defender the expected loss from trial must exceed the cost of settling (assumed to equal the damages involved, £X) to make going to trial worthwhile, i.e., $P < 3/5$. Thus for situations where the nature of the evidence to hand is such as to imply the probability of a successful outcome for the pursuer in the range: $2/5 < P < 3/5$, then trials will occur.

3. In each of the expected outcome matrix entries for the pursuer the calculation is of the expected gain by going to trial, which is:

   $P_w D − (1 − P_w)(C_p + C_d)$

   where,

   P_w = probability of the pursuer winning at trial
   C_p = the costs incurred by the pursuer
   C_d = the costs incurred by the defender

   And for the defender each of the entries reflects his/her expected losses at trial:

   $− (1−P_w)(D + C_p + C_d)$

   As the combination of the costs (C_p, C_d) vary then so does the probability of the pursuer winning.

4. See Rickman and Heyes (1997) for a considered discussion of legal expenses insurance.

Bibliography

Bebchuk, L. A., (1984). 'Litigation and settlement under imperfect information', *Rand Journal of Economics*, **15**, 3; 404–415.

Bowles, R., (1996). 'Reform of legal aid and the solicitor's profession'. *Hume Papers on Public Policy*, **4**, 4; 4–23.

Cooter, R. D., and Rubinfeld, D. L., (1994). 'An economic model of legal discovery'. *Journal of Legal Studies*, **23**; 435–463.

Cooter, R., Marks, S., and Mnookin, R., (1982). 'Bargaining in the shadow of the law: A testable model of strategic behavior', *Journal of Legal Studies*, **11**; 225–251.

Cranston, R., (1995). Zuckerman, A. A. S., and Cranston, R., (eds), 'Research and Access to Justice', in *Reform of Civil Procedure. Essays on 'Access to Justice'*, Oxford: Clarendon Press; 31–59.

Cullen, The Rt. Hon. Lord, (1995). *Review of the business of the Outer House of the Court of Session*. Edinburgh: Scottish Courts Administration.

Fenn, P., and Rickman, N., (1997). 'Delay and settlement in litigation'. Paper presented to the American Law and Economics Association, Toronto.

Fiss, O. M., (1985). 'Against settlement'. *The Yale Law Journal*, **93**, 6; 1073–1090.

Genn, H., (1987). *Hard Bargaining: Out of court settlement in personal injury actions*. Oxford: Oxford University Press.

Goriely, T., (1995). Zuckerman, A. A. S., and Cranston, R., (eds). 'The Government's Legal Aid reforms' in *Reform of Civil Procedure. Essays on 'Access to Justice'*, Oxford: Clarendon Press; 347–369.

Gould, J., (1973). 'The economics of legal conflicts', *Journal of Legal Studies*, **2**, 2; 279–300.

Gravelle, H., (1996). 'What price should be charged for civil justice?', *Hume Papers on Public Policy*, **4**, 4; 36–52.

Gravelle, H., and Waterson, M., (1993). 'No win, no fee: some economics of contingent legal fees', *Economic Journal*, **103**; 1205–1220.

Gray, A., Fenn, P., and Rickman, N., (1996). 'Monitoring legal aid: Back to first principals?', *Hume Papers on Public Policy*, **4**, 4; 4–35.

Halpern, P. J., and Turnbull, S. M., (1982). Evans R. G., and Trebilcock, M. J., (eds). 'An economic analysis of legal fees contracts' in *Lawyers and the Consumer Interest: Regulating the market for legal services*, Toronto: Butterworths; 161–197.

Hay, B., (1997). 'Optimal contingent fees in a world of settlement', *Journal of Legal Studies*, **26**, 1; 259–278.

Hay, B., (1995). 'Effort, information, settlement, trial', *Journal of Legal Studies*, **24**, 1; 29–61.

Hughes, J. W., and Snyder, E. A., (1995). 'Litigation and settlement under the English and American Rules: theory and evidence', *Journal of Law and Economics*, **38**; 225–250.

Hughes, The Rt. Hon. Lord (1980). *Royal Commission on Legal Services in Scotland*. Edinburgh: Her Majesty's Stationery Office.

Hurst, P. T., (1995). **Civil Costs**. London: Sweet & Maxwell.

Kaplow, L., and Shavell, S., (1996). 'Accuracy in the assessment of damages'. *Journal of Law and Economics*, **36**; 191–210.

Katz, A. W., (1997). Bouckaert B., and De Geest G., (eds). 'Indemnity of legal fees' in *Encyclopedia of Law and Economics*. Edward Elgar and the University of Ghent.

Korobkin, R., and Guthrie, C., (1997). 'Psychology, economics, and settlement: a new look at the role of the lawyer'. *Texas Law Review*, **76** (forthcoming).

Kritzer, H. M., (1991). *Let's Make a Deal*. Wisconsin: University of Wisconsin Press.

KPMG Peat Marwick (1994). 'Study on causes of delay in the high court and county courts. Final report'. London: Lord Chancellor's Department.

Landes, W. M., (1971). 'An economic analysis of the courts', *Journal of Law and Economics*, **14**; 61–107.

Mays, R., (1997). 'The changing landscape of dispute resolution', *Hume Papers on Public Policy* **5**, 4 (forthcoming).

Miller, G., (1986). 'An economic analysis of Rule 68', *Journal of Legal Studies*, **15**; 93–125.

Mnookin, R. H., and Kornhauser, L., (1979). 'Bargaining in the shadow of the law: The case if divorce', *The Yale Law Journal*, **88**, 5; 950–997.

Morris, S., and Headrick, D., (1995). *Pilgrim's Process? Defended actions in the Sheriff's Ordinary Court*. Edinburgh: The Scottish Office Central Research Unit.

Murray, A., (1997). 'Fair Notice: the role of written pleadings in the Scottish civil justice system'. *Hume Papers on Public Policy* **5**, 4 (forthcoming).

Ogus, A., (1997). 'Civil procedure reform and economic analysis'. University of Manchester, Law School, Working Paper.
Parratt, D., (1997). 'Access to Justice? Lessons from the Sheriff Court'. *Hume Papers on Public Policy*, **5**, 4 (forthcoming).
Pfenningstorf, W., (1984). 'The European experience with attorney fee shifting', Law and Contemporary Problems, **47**, 1; 37–124.
Plot, C. R., (1987). 'Legal fees: a comparison of the American and English rules'. *Journal of Law, Economics, and Organization*, **3**, 2; 185–192.
P'ng, I. P. L., (1983). 'Strategic behavior in suit, settlement, and trial', *The Bell Journal of Economics*, **14**; 539–550.
Posner, R. A., (1992). *Economic Analysis of Law*, Fourth Edition. Boston: Little Brown and Company.
Posner, R. A., (1973). 'An economic approach to legal procedure and judicial administration', *Journal of Legal Studies*, **2**, 2; 399–458.
Priest, G. L., (1989). 'Private litigants and the court congestion problem', *Boston University Law Review*, **69**; 527–559.
Priest, G. L., (1987). 'Measuring legal change', *Journal of Law, Economics, and Organization*, **3**, 2; 193–225.
Reinganum, J. F., and Wilde, L. L., (1986). 'Settlement, litigation, and the allocation of litigation costs', *Rand Journal of Economics*, **17**, 4; 557–566.
Rickman, N., and Heyes, A., (1997). 'Legal expenses insurance, risk aversion and litigation'. Paper presented at the Annual Conference of the European Law and Economics Association, Barcelona.
Rickman, N., (1997). 'The empirical analysis of litigation: two illustrations from the economics literature'. Paper presented to the Lord Chancellor's Department, London.
Rickman, N., (1996). 'Contingent fees and litigation settlement'. Discussion Paper in Economics, **9**, University of Surrey.
Rickman, N., (1995). Zuckerman, A. A. S., and Cranston, R., (eds). 'The economics of cost shifting rules' in *Reform of Civil Procedure Essays on 'Access to Justice'*. Oxford: Clarendon Press; 327–345.
Shavell, S., (1996). 'The fundamental divergence between the private and the social motive to use the legal system'. Harvard Law School: John M. Ohlin Center for Law, Economics, and Business, Discussion Paper No. 11/96.
Shavell, S., (1995). 'Alternative dispute resolution: an economic analysis', *Journal of Legal Studies*, **24**, 1; 1–28.
Shavell, S., (1982). 'Suit, settlement, and trial: a theoretical analysis under alternative methods for the allocation of legal costs', *Journal of Legal Studies*, **11**; 55–81.
Snyder, E. A., and Hughes, J. W., (1990). 'The English rule for allocating legal costs: evidence confronts theory', *Journal of Law, Economics, and Organization*, **6**, 2; 345–380.
Spier, K. E., (1994). 'Pre-trial bargaining and the design of fee-shifting rules', *Rand Journal of Economics*, **25**, 2; 197–214.
Spier, K. E., (1992). 'The dynamics of pretrial negotiation', *Review of Economic Studies*, **59**; 93–108.
Stephen, F., and Love, J., (1997). 'Regulation of the legal profession: a survey of the theoretical and empirical literature'. University of Strathclyde, Glasgow.
Tiplady, M., (1991). 'Payments into court for plaintiffs', *The Law Society's Gazette*, **30**; 17,20.
Tullock, G., (1980). *Trials on Trial*. New York: Columbia University Press.
Wadia, R., (1997). 'Judicial Case Management. The quiet but significant revolution'. *Hume Papers on Public Policy* **5**, 4 (forthcoming).

Woolf, The Right Honourable, Lord (1995). *Access to Justice. Interim Report.* HMSO, June, London:

Woolf, The Right Honourable, Lord (1996). *Access to Justice. Final Report.* HMSO, July, London.

Zander, M., (1995). Zuckerman A. A. S., and Cranston, R., (eds). 'Why Lord Woolf's proposed reforms of civil litigation should be rejected', in *Reform of Civil Procedure. Essays on 'Access to Justice'*, Oxford: Clarendon Press; 79–95.

Zuckerman, A A .S., (1993). 'Interlocutory remedies in quest of procedural fairness', *The Modern Law Review*, **56**; 325–341.

The Changing Landscape of Dispute Resolution in Scotland

Richard Mays

Introduction

Controversy and disputes are an integral part of the evolution of society (Renfrew 997:145; Moody and Mackay 1995:1). In the post second World War era there has been an expansion of both the extent and nature of disputes (evidenced not least by the dramatic increase in litigation). This situation, though partially fuelled by the advent of Legal Aid ensuring financial accessibility to public dispute resolution mechanisms, is primarily explained by fundamental societal change which has created further interfaces with, and requirements for, dispute resolution mechanisms. The greater prevalence of dysfunctional families and an expansion of individual employment rights are but two examples of how, and why, resort to dispute resolution mechanisms has expanded enormously in the modern era. Added to social change, is a growing consciousness of legal rights and, a more assertive attitude amongst the populace.

Expansion of disputes has brought greater exposure to, and scrutiny of, existing dispute resolution mechanisms; exposure has brought criticism of the current system; and criticism has fuelled a quest for reform, change and alternatives. Scotland, in common with other civilised nations, has been catalysed by the forces of change and as a consequence can be said to be in a transitional and dynamic phase of civil justice reform. Traditional dispute resolution mechanisms – litigation and arbitration – have come under challenge from the relatively modern concept of Alternative Dispute Resolution. In responding to considerable dissatisfaction with aspects of traditional dispute resolution mechanisms and the perceived threat of ADR, both litigation and arbitration have undergone, and are undergoing change. Procedures in both Scottish civil courts have been subjected to some form of change in the past few years and indeed, there are further proposals in respect of both courts.

What follows is a discussion of those changes, as well as discussion of ADR in Scotland and an attempt at some analysis of the key features and themes of the changing vista of dispute resolution in Scotland in the 1990s. Any discussion must be prefaced with an acknowledgement that both the forces of change and the process of change are not uniquely domiciled in Scotland. As one surveys the literature, one becomes struck by the fact that many of the key issues and drivers of reform are drawn from experience and practice in other jurisdictions, most notably England and America. There should be no surprise in that fact. Despite its muddled place in legal jurisdictions, and the many influences that have fashioned modern Scots Law, it is relatively uncontroversial to contend that in dispute resolution, Scotland displays common law technique. That fact alone justifies looking to the literature of the common law jurisdictions. If any other justification is needed, it is in the scarcity, and relative poverty of our own literature on the subject of civil justice reform.

Reform of Scottish Civil Court Procedures

Sheriff Court

Discussion of the sheriff court procedure is encumbered by the fact that there are three distinct procedures in operation – small claims procedure, summary cause procedure and ordinary cause procedure (ignoring the technicality that small claims procedure is a variant of summary cause procedure). In the past few years ordinary cause procedure in the Sheriff Court has undergone dramatic reconstruction. In contrast the two other procedures have remained relatively stable. That stability may shortly be challenged. The Sheriff Court Rules Council (the statutory body charged with keeping the rules under constant review) are known to be considering changes to both the Small Claims Rules (introduced in 1988) and the Summary Cause Procedure (implemented in 1976 and last revised in 1990, see Mays 1996). Summary Cause and Small Claims are related procedures. Their primary objective is to provide less formalised and relatively inexpensive procedures for disputes involving lower level pecuniary sums. In the case of Small Claims the upper financial limit is £750; whilst summary cause procedure is restricted to £1500.

Despite being in existence since 1976, much of the early gloss of the summary cause procedure has been diminished following the inception of the small claims rules in 1988. Of all the civil court procedures, summary cause has proved relatively durable. The original intention was that the procedure would provide a quick, speedy and efficient method of resolving disputes at the lower end of the pecuniary scale (Mays 1995:1–3). It was the Grant Committee Report on the Sheriff Court (1967 Cmnd 3248:6.11) which had asserted 'that there should be a standard summary procedure, which should largely assimilate actions to the existing small debt procedure and would not resemble ordinary procedure'. The rules developed under the Sheriff Courts (Scotland) Act 1971 were implemented in 1976. Since that time there have been 5 occasions when the rules have been amended. The Procedure has not been the subject of fundamental review in 20 years. There may be various reasons why there has been no wholesale change in this procedure. Firstly, the development of the Small Claims Procedure in 1988 (see below) attempted to deal with much of the criticism that summary cause procedure might have attracted had it continued as the sole means of resolving small debts. Excessive legalism, formality and lawyer domination are obvious points of reference for detractors. Secondly, the process of review of all Sheriff Court procedures is undertaken by a statutory body, the Sheriff Court Rules Council. That particular body has been engaged in a considerable programme of work especially over the past decade. The development of new Ordinary Cause Rules (see below) and the current work framing court rules to cater for the revolutionary Children (Scotland) Act 1995 have undoubtedly slowed the process of reform. Alternatively, it may well be, as the writer has suggested previously (Mays 1995:182), that the procedure has endured primarily because its works rather well. In contending this, one must accept that there are flaws in the system. Even were the Sheriff Court Rules Council minded to retain the existing summary cause procedure, there are clear deficiencies in the procedure which will require to be addressed (see Mays 1996).

The secrecy surrounding the process of review by the Sheriff Court Rules Council make it impossible to determine what the future holds for both procedures. Any prognostication on what is likely to happen to both Summary Cause and Small Claims must, by definition, be viewed as 'crystal ball gazing'. It is hardly incisive to suggest that the Sheriff Court Rules Council will either elect to reform existing procedures retaining the essentials of both, or attempt to rejoin both procedures into a single procedure summary in nature intended to be at one speedy, informal, litigant friendly and efficient in terms of time and cost. How simple a reunification process might be is difficult to gauge. There are clearly features of both procedures which command respect and merit. A unitary procedure with twin tracks might provide the answer. More complex disputes might be resolved in the higher track, whilst relatively minor disputes may be resolved in a distilled version of the more formal procedure. The route a case may take might be resolved at a preliminary hearing conducted in similar fashion to that existing in the small claims procedure. There is nothing novel in this type of approach; dual track procedure is evident in both the new Ordinary Cause procedure in the Sheriff Court and the proposals of Lord Cullen for the Outer House of the Court of Session (both discussed below). Whatever the ultimate course reform takes, it is envisaged that some form of procedure, summary in nature, will be retained. Indeed, the writer predicts that such a summary procedure will take in a much expanded volume of litigation. The current pecuniary maximum for summary cause is £1500; there seems no real reason why that ceiling should not be lifted to around £10,000. Admittedly, pecuniary value does not always equate with legal complexity but, as long as there exists flexibility to transfer cases to higher levels in the procedural hierarchy in meritorious cases, then one can set such arbitrary financial limits.

The Ordinary Cause procedure of the Sheriff Court was substantially reformed in 1993 (see Mays 1997:93–101). Research (Morris and Headrick 1995) disclosed considerable delay, repeated callings in court and the fact that only five percent of cases proceeded to proof hearings. The response of the Sheriff Court Rules Council was that 'new procedures were needed which would avoid unnecessary complexity, and which would provide a proper procedural basis for the effective and economical management of cases once parties have embarked on litigation' (Sheriff Principal Hay, Chairman of the Sheriff Court Rules Council quoted in Mays 1997:93–4). The framing of the new procedural rules followed five basic principle set by the Sheriff Court Rules Council. Firstly, cases should only call in court when necessary; secondly, the number of calling should be kept to a minimum; thirdly, there should be set time limits for completion of each stage of the procedure; fourthly, control and management of litigation should be vested in the court not the litigants; and finally there was an attempt to harmonise sheriff court procedure with that of the Court of Session.

The new procedure contained many interesting departures from what had gone before (see Mays 1997:94–101). Several key developments can be singled out for special attention. Central among all the reforms are undoubtedly the strict time-tabling of the procedure and the newly developed options hearing (see Neilson 1993) where Sheriffs determine the ensuing route the litigation will follow. The Sheriff may determine that a case should proceed to debate, proof or, in complex cases proceed by way of an extended additional procedure. Early preparation is encouraged by various new rules in the procedure. The strict time-tabling and ability to engage in more formalised managerialism by sheriffs represents the first formalised case-management system within the Sheriff Court. Sheriffs in the past have intervened to varying degrees; what is novel in the new procedure is that this is no longer a matter left to the vagaries of judicial discretion and demeanour. It is now a formalised requirement of all Sheriffs (see Andrew Welsh Ltd v Thornehome Services 1994 SCLR 1021 (Sh.Ct); Mays 1997:96; Mays 1998). Naturally, the extent to which sheriffs have sought to fulfil their new found obligations has been variable. The writer has previously cast doubt on some of the petty managerialism of some judges (see Mays 1997:97–101). Some fairly trenchant stances have been adopted by sheriffs in an attempt to reform practitioner attitudes to the process of litigation following the introduction of the new rules; the extent to which this has been fully successful must be dubious. Expectation that wholesale reformation of long established attitudes to litigation could be achieved in such a short space of time, was doubtless ambitious.

The new interventionist strategies introduced by the new rules have not been universally welcomed (Mays 1997:96) primarily on the basis that it is neutral interference into a private dispute. It is taking time to develop understanding that private disputes brought into the public forum of the courts, and utilising public funds in the process, are no longer in the 'ownership' of the parties. Acceptance of this will go a long way to smoothing the path for more formalised case management in the future and the prevention of abuses of the litigation process both in terms of squandering public resources and utilising it as a coercive forum against one's opponent. In the atmosphere of managerialism and procedural skirmishes, the ultimate goal of substantive justice may either be lost or substantially obscured. Procedural justice naturally is part of substantive justice but not the dominant part. It remains imperative that in the search for procedural efficiency, that substantive justice is of primary importance in any method of dispute resolution. All too often in dealing with our court procedures there is a tendency to be inflective towards procedural issues to the detriment of awareness that behind all the procedural niceties there are litigants [often individuals] who simply want a fair hearing and determination of their dispute.

Court of Session Procedure

Lord Cullen's Review

Procedure in the superior civil court of first instance in Scotland has also come under some scrutiny. The recent review undertaken by Lord Cullen and the new rules introduced for commercial causes both in the Outer House are worthy of comment. Lord Cullen's remit was 'to review the manner in which business in the Outer House is administered, conducted and allocated with a view to making recommendations as to the improvement' and specifically to assess whether there should be greater case-management, simplification of procedure either by changing rules of procedure or the practice of pleading, and consider how to expedite progress of litigation. The research undertaken by Lord Cullen into existing practice in the Court of Session disclosed problems similar to those identified in the Morris and Headrick research into the Sheriff Court (Cullen 1995:3.12–3.14). Lord Cullen was critical of aspects of the pleading system operating in Scotland. He criticises over-elaboration of detail in pleadings, lack of candour in defences, undue reliance on points of pleading prejudicial to justice in the case, that the system of pleading is unduly elaborate especially in simpler cases, and a failure to give notice to the courts of the issues (Mays 1997:103). With this in mind Lord Cullen recommends a system of abbreviated pleadings representing a 'mid-point between those who have argued for abolition of pleadings altogether and the status quo' (Morrison 1996:94–5; Upton 1996:111–2). Lord Cullen's other approach, analogous to that suggested by Lord Woolf in England, is to have alternative track procedure depending on the complexity of the case before the court. Cases deemed meritorious by the judge would proceed to full pleadings identical to the existing arrangements whereas, ordinary run of the mill cases would be constrained within a restricted pleading system. Unlike Woolf, Lord Cullen's proposal for access to the fuller (and hence more costly procedure) would depend not on financial value differentials but on the issue of legal complexity.

Of major significance in the Cullen proposals for the Outer House are those relating to the adoption of formalised case-management and the re-introduction of pre-proof hearings (Upton 1996:112–3; Morrison 1996:96–8; Mays 1998). Like most case management systems the intention is to tighten the utilisation of resources and to transfer power from the litigants to the court itself. Expedition of the case and the avoidance of unnecessary expense would be key aims of such hearings (Cullen 1995:6.19, 6.31). The case-management hearing would take place in all actions at the end of the adjustment period and in this sense can be equiperated with the options hearing in the sheriff court Ordinary Cause hearing. The re-introduction of pre-proof hearings represents further evidence of the intention to constrain the parties' use of the resource of the court and to ensure that parties are expediting their case in an appropriate manner. The intention may also be to concentrate the minds of the parties in respect of settlement prior to the proof. At pre-proof hearings it is proposed that the court may intervene to compel the parties to undertake further course of action to prepare for the ensuing proof hearing.

Commercial Causes

Following the Report of the Working Party on Commercial Causes (1993) under the Chairmanship of Lord Coulsfield, a new regime was introduced in the Court of Session for dealing with such actions. The new procedure represented a radical departure. According to Clancy, Murray and Wadia (1997:45) the new procedural rules were 'the first conscious attempt in Scotland to implement whole scale management measures with fully fledged judicial proactivity'. The Working Party recorded the two perennial complaints of excessive cost and delay but to these it added a third – a lack of judicial expertise. Clancy, Murray and Wadia (1997:47) describe the essence of the scheme as designed 'to manage cases through three principal types of hearing – preliminary hearings, procedural hearings and hearings for final disposal. The emphasis is on selecting procedures to suit the requirements of individual cases'. Essentially, there is an attempt to ration procedure. There are various novel aspects of the procedure – the insistence of continuity with the same judge hearing all procedural aspects of a particular case, the downgrading in importance of written pleadings with the court identifying the key legal issues (and as a consequence ordering adjustment of pleadings accordingly), the promotion of early disclosure without recourse to commission and diligence orders, parties might be asked to lodge statements of facts on particular issues, the allowance of proof hearings only once the court is satisfied that the case is both ready to proceed to that stage and that it is appropriate.

The Commercial Cause Procedure rules in the Court of Session differ from the proposals advanced by Lord Cullen in two material respects. Those are a more intensive form of case management throughout the procedure rather than strategic points and, secondly, the variation of treatment of written pleadings. It remains to be seen whether the commercial cause rules will continue in their current form if the proposals by Lord Cullen are adopted. Clancy, Murray and Wadia (1997:57) take the view that there should be retention of a separate commercial action procedure.

The Court of Session process reform continues to be detached from that in the sheriff court. As a consequence the piecemeal haphazard process of reform of civil litigation procedures continues without any evident sign of strategic assessment of the essential qualities to be enshrined in those systems. 'Doing their own thing' is not the only insularity in the system; the process of reform remains essentially in the hands of the suppliers rather than the consumers. One wonders how much longer will the public entrust that process of reform to those who have the greatest vested interest in it?

Arbitration

Arbitration has a long and distinguished history in Scots Law as a method of dispute resolution (see Hunter 1987:22–58). Once seen as an 'alternative' dispute resolution mechanism, it has in the opinion of the writer been all but subsumed as a traditional form of dispute resolution. Morgan defines 'arbitration' as 'the judicial resolution of a dispute . . . by an independent person (an arbiter) who may be selected by the disputants or on their behalf on the basis of his experience, reputation and expertise in the subject matter of the dispute and in then law, practice and procedure of arbitration' (1993:24). The transition from 'alternative' to 'traditional' can accordingly be sustained on the basis long history, the arbitrary nature of the process and legalism involved. To define arbitration as 'traditional' is not to denigrate it or to deny the fact that it provides an alternative to litigation as a means of resolving disputes. The continuing appeal of arbitration, particularly to commercial disputants is undoubtedly the introduction of a skilful arbiter and arguably the cheaper financial cost. This latter point is of some dubiety and the notion that arbitration is cheaper than litigation must be qualified (see Moody and Mackay 1995:78). Morgan has suggested that arbitration is cheaper than litigation provided the parties want to resolve the dispute and that the lawyers involve exhibit knowledge, flexibility and restraint in their use of resources (1993:27). Not all commentators discount the notion that arbitration is a form of ADR. According to Davidson 'Arbitration is arguably the form of ADR which most closely resembles ordinary court processes and indeed, certain arbitrations mirror that process almost exactly, and while arbitration can permit of considerable procedural flexibility, it is in essence an adversarial and adjudicatory process' (1993:22). Certainly, with the advent of newer forms of dispute resolution such as mediation the trend is to view arbitration as traditional.

The period immediately before the advent of the 1990s was punctuated with considerable activity in the field of Arbitration Law. The Lord Advocate established the Scottish Advisory Committee on Arbitration Law in 1986. The remit of the committee was

(a) To advise on whether, and if so to what extent, the provisions of the draft Model Law (on International Commercial Arbitration) adopted by a Working Group of the United Nations Commission on International Trade Law in February 1984 should be implemented in Scotland and what measures should be taken for this purpose.

(b) To examine the operation of the system of arbitration in Scotland in the light of the Model Law and to make recommendations regarding any legislative or other steps which the committee consi'ers should be taken to improve the system of arbitration in Scotland.

This Committee in conjunction with the Departmental Advisory Committee on Arbitration Law published a joint consultation paper on the Model Law. Consequently, the Model Law was adopted into Scots law by section 66 and Schedule 7 of the Law Reform (Miscellaneous Provisions) (Scotland) Act

1990. In addition to a transformation of the law, there was an expansion of the provision of arbitration services and increased interest in the subject by various professional bodies. These various developments prompted Davidson to enthuse that 'these are times of great significance for arbitration. A great many individuals and organisations clearly regard it as a subject of some importance. The process of change begun in the 1980s has continued into the 1990s. Considerable public resources have been devoted to investigating the case for reform of arbitration law' (Davidson 1993:1). Despite that investment, arbitration reform has been overshadowed by court procedural reform and the advent of ADR. Interestingly, Davidson's empirical research pointed to a growing awareness of arbitration and 'its advantages (real or perceived) as a dispute resolving mechanism'. However a small group of respondents to Davidson's study noted a decline in arbitration 'because it was increasingly seen as an anachronism, more expensive and less practical than other forms of dispute resolution, tending to replicate court procedures and just as slow as going to court, involving lawyers to too great an extent, and unsuitable for multi-party disputes' (1993:7).

One of the key problems of arbitration is Davidson's conclusion that 'much of the map remains blank' (1993:21). Equally importantly, he astutely noted that it would be improper to assess arbitration 'without confronting the fundamental question of whether arbitration is the most appropriate form of ADR to support'. Whilst recognising the undoubted threat of commercial mediation to traditional arbitration processes, it is apparent that traditional sectors of arbitration practice are remaining loyal to this method of resolving disputes. Commercial mediation is yet to see any meaningful activity (see Mays and Clark 1996; Moody and Mackay 1995:151–8).

One of the major criticisms of arbitration in the modern era is excessive legalism (see Murray 1997). In The Antios [1985] AC 191 Lord Roskill had posited that 'One purpose of arbitration, especially in commercial disputes, is the avoidance of delays traditionally if often unfairly associated with the judicial process. The award of the arbitral tribunal can, it is supposed, be obtained swiftly and simply without elaboration. Unhappily, the former virtually unrestricted right to demand a special case from arbitral tribunals, made these admirable objectives almost impossible of attainment. The arbitral process became even more protracted than the judicial' (quoted in Murray 1997:64). The key problem is the relative ease of judicial intervention. Murray identifies the problem as one where 'Enmeshing the essentially independent and private arbitral process, of its nature intended to produce a final and binding decision, with a hierarchical judicial structure, offers enormous potential for abuse' (1997:65). Recent judicial pronouncements have indicated a desire on the part of the courts to detach themselves from the process of arbitration as much as possible (see K/S A/S Bill Biakh v Hyundai Corporation [1988] 1 Lloyds Rep 187 per Steyn J:189; ERDC Construction Ltd v HM Love and Co (No 2) 1997 SLT 175 per Lord President Hope:178). Murray says 'It is commonplace in certain types of arbitration in Scotland that the arbiter is not a lawyer, though he may have the assistance of a lawyer as clerk. But the parties will be legally represented; and the corollary all too often is that at the behest of the parties' legal representatives the procedure follows a course very similar to that of a civil litigation' (1997:66).

Arbitration in Scotland stands at a relatively dynamic stage of its development. Consideration is ongoing as to whether a statutory framework should be sought for Scottish arbitration. The UNCITRAL Model has been adopted for international arbitration. In addition UNCITRAL may be deployed voluntarily for domestic arbitration. The various options for reform have been extensively canvassed (Davidson 1989a; Davidson 1989b; Davidson 1989c; Dervaird 1997). In respect of the future framework, Davidson seems clear '[t]he solution must indeed be an all embracing statutory statement of Scots arbitration law with the Model Law at its core'.

In another comment Davidson has contended 'there is no good reason why the Model Law should not apply to both domestic and international arbitration'. He describes Scots law of arbitration as 'obscure, uncertain, defective or positively inimical to good arbitration practice. Thus the inadequacies of our domestic law could undermine the effectiveness of the Model Law and diminish the attractiveness of Scotland as a forum for international commercial arbitration. The solution must indeed be an all embracing statutory statement of Scots arbitration law with the Model Law as its core' (1989:218).

The Scottish Advisory Committee on Arbitration Law submitted a report to the Lord Advocate in March 1996. The basic approach of the committee is that 'in recognition of the private consensual characteristics of the arbitral process, the courts should be able to intervene only to the extent necessary to ensure fairness of the process' (consultation paper on legislation for domestic arbitration in Scotland, Scottish Courts Administration, 1997:1) The report does not recommend the development of a comprehensive statutory framework for domestic arbitration similar to that operative in England and Wales under the Arbitration Act 1996. Instead the proposed legislation seeks to compliment voluntarily agreed arrangements between the parties. The proposed Arbitration Bill for Scotland contains four strands. There are provisions which address preliminary problems in arbitrations e.g. the failure to specify the number of arbitrators (section 2), failure to agree on arbitrators (section 4). Secondly there are provisions which relate to the powers of the arbitral tribunal and related arbitration practice matters, e.g. power to award interest and damages (Clause 22 and 24), power to make interim awards (Clause 23). Thirdly, there are provisions designed to protect the interests of the parties, e.g. the introduction of time limits for completion of procedural matters (Clauses 8, 9 and 15) and the power to correct errors in awards (clause 26). Finally, there are provisions which seek to define more explicitly the role of the courts in arbitration, e.g. the power to set aside awards in whole or in part because of misconduct by a member of a tribunal (Clause 10). Significantly, amongst these provisions is a clause which repeals the existing provision for appeal by stated case (Clause 29). Such a proposal were it adopted would lead to a re-alignment with England and Wales. Appeal by stated case was introduced in Scotland in 1972 (by Section 3 of Administration (Scotland) Act 1972) but abolished in England and Wales in 1979 (by the Arbitration Act 1979).

The UNCITRAL model which was introduced into Scots law by Sections 66 and 67 of the Law Reform (Miscellaneous Provisions) (Scotland) Act 1990 would be re-enacted as Schedule 1 to the proposed Bill. The proposal is (in Clause 33) that the new Act will only apply to arbitration's entered into after the commencement of the act unless the parties agree otherwise.

The proposed Bill does not address the issue of Geneva Convention on the Execution of Foreign Arbitral Awards 1927 (introduced into Scots law under Part II of the Arbitration Act 1950) or the New York Convention on the Execution of Foreign Arbitral Awards 1958 (introduced under the Arbitration Act 1975). Views are being sought as to whether foreign arbitral awards qualifying under these Conventions should continue to be recognised in Scotland. These latter proposals have all the hallmarks of simply being tidying-up proposals.

The process of arbitration continues to interest many parties. Its problems emanate in its relationship with the courts and the legal profession. Once proffered as a real alternative to litigation, it is now attracting criticism similar to that bedevilling litigation processes and in the process is being seen as a 'traditional' process. The advent of new ADR methodology, particularly commercial mediation, may place further pressure on arbitration particularly in the context of reformation of court procedures. Recent reforms and discussions in arbitration law point to a healthy period of self-reflection in this sphere. The willingness to respond to the changing landscape of dispute resolution can only be beneficial.

Alternative Dispute Resolution

With general dissatisfaction and rising cost, it is hardly surprising that 'alternatives' to traditional dispute resolution mechanism have come into vogue. A concept originating in America in the 1970s, 'ADR is . . . a portmanteau term comprehending a diverse range of dispute resolution processes, any one of which can have nothing in common with another than the fact that they form 'alternatives' to civil litigation' (Davidson 1993:22). Adler and Morris (1996) refer to 'ADR' as an 'ill-defined and contested concept'. ADR is not only of interest to the non-legal community; even those responsible for the administration of justice have displayed an interest in it (Adler and Morris 1996:2). Renfrew (1997:146–7) suggests that ADR may be classified in three ways. Firstly, whether it is a private process; secondly whether it is an adjudicative process; and finally whether it is rights based or interest based. Whilst Brown and Marriot view ADR as complimentary to litigation and other adjudicatory forms of justice 'providing processes which can either stand in their own right or be used as an adjunct to adjudication' (1993:13). In Scotland the predominant ADR process is mediation.

Interestingly, as Adler and Morris (1996:3) note 'many of the "alternatives" to litigation which proponents of ADR have advocated have either been used to modify "traditional" forms of litigation or have been grafted on to them. The continuing essence of "alternativeness" must be questionable. The incoherence in conception of ADR undoubtedly operates as a barrier to fuller understanding and development of the subject (Mays and Clark 1996). The perceived mutuality of benefit stands at the heart of common understandings of ADR. For example Fuller (1991) contends 'ADR is always directed towards bringing about a more harmonious relationship between the parties, whether this be agreed through explicit agreement, through a reciprocal acceptance of the "social norms" relevant to their relationship, or simply because the parties have been helped to a new and more perceptive understanding of one another's problems'.

Whilst there is increased support for ADR in the USA (see Renfrew 1997: 149–152), here in Scotland, ADR practice is rather patchy (Mays and Clark 1996; Moody and Mackay 1995:3). Of the spheres of dispute resolution, only family law offers evidence of widespread activity of mediation practice. In the commercial, consumer and community fields the level of activity is quite poor. The reasons for such inactivity are varied and in some cases uncertain. Suggestions have been made that there needs to be greater public awareness, less lawyer hostility, greater court referrals, and a change in public attitude (Mays and Clark 1996; Moody and Mackay 1995:151–8). There is also uncertainty as to whether ADR processes will be any cheaper than traditional dispute resolution mechanisms (Ogus 1996). Such bald financial considerations ignore longer term social benefits to be derived from more harmonious methods of dispute resolution.

In all probability, if ADR is to prosper adequate and sustained external funding will need to be made available for ADR processes, either by the State or through other private means (Clark and Mays 1997). If state funding is to be available for ADR processes, policy makers will require to be convinced of its cost-benefit balance. In our current state of understanding, detailing the costs is problematic; the benefits in financial terms are equally vague. Arguments further based on social benefits will doubtless be confronted with the charge of being unquantifiable, intangible and nebulous.

There is very little regulation of ADR either in Scotland or the UK (Clark and Mays 1996; Moody and Mackay 1995:159). The extent to which ADR need be subjected to external regulatory control has been hotly debated (Raitt 1995; Greatbach and Dingwall 1993). Clark (1996) has suggested ADR processes would benefit from one unified regulatory body designed to protect participants from 'negligent, incompetent and unscrupulous ADR practice' and, at the same time provide a body to co-ordinating education and training and to regulate ADR activity generally. Currently, in Scotland, as in the rest of the UK the limited regulation that exists is sporadic and haphazard. Currently limited regulation exists in the form of codes of practice and professional standards set by accrediting bodies for mediators (Clark and Mays 1996). There are some attempts at standardisation, particularly by UK College of Family Mediators. However the landscape is bedevilled by professional and organisational rivalries. As ADR grows the pressure for regulation will intensify; that pressure will be particularly significant if ADR becomes enmeshed in legal procedures.

The relationship between ADR and the courts is an uneasy one. The suggestion that mediation plays no part in state mechanisms for dispute resolution, is no longer tenable. There are various instances where ADR plays a limited part in the court procedures (see Moody and Mackay 1995; Mays and Clark 1997:60–1). It seems likely that there will continue to be a convergence and interdependence between ADR and traditional forms of dispute resolution. The extent to which mediation and other forms of ADR can be viewed as 'alternative' is questionable. ADR, on current assessment, is unlikely to be imperialist and supplant litigation; the likelihood is that ADR processes will follow a dual path as, on the one hand, a stand alone private or public dispute resolution mechanism and, on the other, become a process enmeshed within re-invented and re-invigorated state litigation systems. In respect of the latter point, there is clear anecdotal support from practitioners and other interested parties for referral of all forms of disputes from the courts to ADR processes (Mays and Clark 1997:62–65).

Civil Justice – a discussion

There are those who overplay the importance and significance of civil justice in society. There are commentators only too willing to view civil justice as the only litmus test of the value of society. At best civil justice is but one test of civilisation. If that much is conceded we can view comments such as those by Professor Hamson (quoted in Jolowicz 1988:7) in an appropriate light. He says '[I]t is in its legal institutions that the characteristics of a civilised country are most clearly revealed, not only and not so much in its substantive law as in its practice and procedure of its courts. Legal procedure is a . . . ritual of extreme social significance. If we can appreciate the meaning of this ritual in the case of our own and even one other community, we can obtain a remarkable insight into the fundamental and largely unformulated beliefs accepted by, and acceptable to, those societies; we begin to understand their collective and perhaps contrasted sense of what is just and fair'.

Adopting Hamson's model, what does one learn about Scottish society from our civil justice system. Essentially, we must concede to being combative and adversarial. It was Couture (1950:7) who contended that 'the civil action is civilisation's substitute for vengeance'. Jolowicz (1988:3) has interpreted this as meaning a form of judicial duel which conceptually underpins the adversary system within the UK. Jolowicz himself challenges the continuation of the combative analogy pointing out that the spontaneity and surprise element associated with combat has been somewhat displaced in the modern procedures of litigation (see Jolowicz 1988:4–5; also Lord Wilberforce in Davies v Eli Lilly and Co [1987] 1 WLR 428:431–2) wherein there may be no contest at all until the party's position is revealed to the court. The imagery of aggression and combat remains powerful nonetheless.

Current discussion of civil justice has been punctuated with several key concerns. Principal amongst those concerns has been the very essence and nature of adversary approach to settling disputes. There are calls for more consensual approaches to dispute resolution. Costs, delay and procedural waste continue to be perennial problems and this had led to call for a 'rationing' of procedure and formalised case management. These combined concerns have also led to pressure for wholesale review of our civil justice system. Given the level of change and the continuing level of dissatisfaction, a fundamental review may indeed become irresistible.

Adversary nature of system

Zuckerman (1995:58) suggests that participants perceive that justice in the adversarial system requires that they be allowed to conduct their case as they see fit. Leaving aside criticisms of the avowedly confrontational nature of such an approach, there is an obvious procedural waste of resources. Despite this, both Lord Woolf (in England) and Lord Cullen (in Scotland) indicate a preference for retention of the adversarial system in their respective spheres. In both reports there is no articulation of an intellectual rationale for such stances. The comments in both Reports represent bald statements which on the face of things seem more intent on reassuring traditionalist opinion than offering underscored support for the concept. Indeed more than one commentator has seen fit to challenge Lord Woolf's implicit view that the adversary system stands unaltered in the onslaught of the 'new' managerialism of case-management (see Jolowicz 1996). Clearly, in Scotland, the Cullen report suffers from the same limited analysis. No one, Lord Cullen included, has yet addressed the implications for the adversarial system in the context of case-management. The problem is explained by an English commentator 'While the English system still clings to a formal adherence to the adversary model, a slow erosion of some of the basic characteristics has taken place in response to the demands of modern litigation and the pressure on public funds. A transition to a more interventionist and regulatory role in relation to the parties has been presented as a vindication of the integrity of the procedural system . . .' (Glasser 1993). As Jolowicz identifies, the issue revolves around how one defines 'adversarial' (1996:199). If it simply means that the parties define the dispute and the courts decide on the sole basis of information supplied by the parties, then clearly case-management does not displace adversarialism. However, the available literature and the underlying ethos in these principal reports both north and south of the border point to a more expansive interventionist approach by the judiciary. In this context, the adversary system, must by definition, be under some strain.

As indicated another key criticism of the adversary system is its confrontational nature. Jaconelli suggests that the common law systems do appear to encourage compromise awards by the courts (what he terms a Solomonic judgment) and systems are imbued with winner takes all mentalities (1992:480). Does the winner-takes-it-all attitude enshrined in courts re-enforce the reluctance to compromise? Certainly, the promoters of ADR (and mediation in particular), point to consensuality as a positive plus in dispute resolution.

Cost and delay

Cost and delay continue to be the principle concerns with modern dispute resolution (Zuckerman 1995:155). There has been a long held desire on the part of the state to limit expenditure on civil justice generally and civil legal aid particularly (Marriott 1995:126). Expense is a problem at all levels of litigation but there are dangers in concentrating on the twin evils of cost and delay especially as the expense of fundamentals (Jolowicz 1988). There are various factors in the spiralling cost of civil litigation, not least the 'Rolls-Royce' standard of legal service and lawyers own self interest in 'milking' the system. Procedures seem capable of absorbing ever increasing sums of money. Zuckerman is surely correct in asserting that, (1995:157) 'we need to fashion an overall strategy which takes account of the potential interaction between different aspects of the system. There would be little point, for instance, in simplifying procedure unless we also remove the incentives for increasing the complexity and duration of litigation. Similarly, it would be self-defeating to speed up the rate of case disposal, if this were going to produce an exponential increase in the volume of litigation that could overwhelm the courts'.

Zuckerman (1995:163–4) also talks of a racheting-up mechanism in civil court procedures. Legally-aided litigants want commensurate standards of legal service as their well-funded opponents have, lawyers fees have increased, the indemnity rule whereby litigants ordinarily reimburse the costs of the winning litigant all contribute to spiralling costs. Litigants undoubtedly perceive that if they spend more their prospects of success will be enhanced. Zuckerman also offers the prospect that the poorer litigant may be able to dictate the procedure; in effect choosing the cheaper option thus inhibiting the wealthier litigant's opportunity for exploitation of the procedure. Wertheimer has also railed against the inequality of legal resources and its likely inegalitarian impact both in litigation procedures and extra-judicial settlement. Parties are all too aware that what they spend on litigation will often influence the outcome of their dispute (Ogus 1996). Lawyers, as much as litigants, are blamed for spiralling costs. According to one commentator 'no measure of procedural simplification, streamlining and judicial intervention would have lasting effects as long as lawyers have an incentive to complicate and protract litigation' (Zuckerman 1995:175; see Ogus 1996). In Scotland, Lord Gill has endorsed the view that expense in the system is in part generated by the provision of the opportunity for financial exploitation by lawyers (1995:131). Movement towards fixed scale fees linked to the value of the claim rather than the time expended may prove one solution. It has also been suggested that the solution may lie in revisiting the indemnification rule of civil procedure or at least limiting litigation costs perhaps to that expended by the loser.

Reform of procedure and rationing of procedure

It has been argued that strategies 'should aim to husband procedural resources so that access to procedure, as distinct from access to the court, would be allowed in proportion to the importance and complexity of disputes' (Zuckerman 1995:180). Zuckerman (1995:158) contends that 'when procedural resources are finite, we should ration their employment and not . . . restrict access to court by means of prohibitive costs'. He suggests a trifurcated approach – cheaper and simpler procedure, incentives to lawyers and clients to keep costs down, and counteraction on the likelihood of greater accessibility to justice (see Zuckerman 1995:15).

Some contend that in an adversarial system it is perfectly legitimate to exploit the procedural devices that the law provides. The usefulness of these devices must vary from case to case and '[j]ust as not all medical conditions require the employment of all the available diagnostic methods, so not all disputes in the courts justify the use of all pre-trial tactics' (Zuckerman 1995:159).

According to Zuckerman, the state does not have an obligation to provide the most accurate civil procedure irrespective of how much it costs (1995:160). We are 'entitled to expect procedures which strive to provide a reasonable measure of protection of rights, commensurable with the resources that we can afford to spend on the administration of justice' (Zuckerman 1995:160-1). The system of necessity must make the compromise but within the economic straitjacket procedural reform is both possible and necessary. Focus can be on economies which do not compromise accuracy and speed of justice. Accuracy may have to be diminished at the expense of speed (Zuckerman 1995:162).

Systems invariably offer considerable scope for protraction and complexity. Part of that problem lies in the fact that procedures must cater for an extremely diverse range of disputes. The objective must be for the full procedural complexity to be deployed only in the most complex of cases. Currently, even the flimsiest of cases permits access to the full range of procedural. Zuckerman, argues that the threshold of an arguable case is set too low (1995:167).

One approach is to direct cases to particular procedures with flexibility for interchange – what Zuckerman calls a rationing of rules (Zuckerman 1995:168-170). The current Scottish System in the Sheriff Court does precisely that, and Lord Cullen's proposals for the Court of Session envisage a dual track system of procedure based on complexity.

The relationship between the appropriateness of procedure and the cost of litigation has been identified in England where Lord Woolf argues for procedure and the associated cost to be 'proportionate to the nature of the issues involved' (Woolf 1995:3; Ogus 1996). In Scotland, the connection has not been explicitly canvassed. However, in choosing a forum for resolution of their disputes 'it is a reasonable inference that their [parties] choice will, to a certain extent, depend on how they trade off the quality of the different services against the price charged' (Ogus 1996:2). However market forces play a limited part in such choice primarily because only one system of resolving disputes has the inherent coercive power of the state at its disposal.

In any new civil justice system it will be important to have a range of options appropriate to the needs of the parties. Directing appropriate cases to particular mechanisms may contain difficulties; there will require to be mixture of voluntarism and coercion as to the path a dispute follows. Where the state is asked to underscore the resources necessary for the settlement of the dispute, it is not unrealistic to suppose it should within reason direct parties to appropriate mechanisms for dispute resolution under the guise of strong managerial judges. Any system which attempts to develop appropriate dispute resolution will naturally require to retain links between the menu of alternatives for resolving disputes to ensure flexibility.

Managerialism and case-management

The rationing of access to procedure will doubtless be influenced by the new managerialism of judges. However not all commentators are convinced that case management will reap the benefits expected of it. 'Given the culture of the legal profession and of the judiciary, Professor Zander is right to doubt whether the mere assumption of a managerial role would lead to the desired reduction in costs or delay' (Zuckerman 1995:172).

Courts have hitherto displayed a leniency in lax attitudes to litigation. Zuckerman argues that 'a managerial policy will not bear the desired fruit unless it is guided by a well articulated policy of rationing procedural resources and is buttressed by specific rules that promote this policy. This would require a cultural change and a material change in procedure' (1995:172–3). Judges must see themselves as managers of scarce public resources. Lord Gill argues strongly for transference of control of the pace of litigation to the courts and out of the hands of the parties and their lawyers. Implicit in Lord Gill's critique of the system is the notion that judges are spending far too long on procedural issues and procedural justice and 'to the extent that such stresses limit a judge's efficiency and creativity, the system of civil justice impaired' (1995:131). A similar view was expressed immediately prior to the introduction of the new sheriff court Ordinary Cause Rules.

Case-management entails not only time-tabling but detailed supervision. In the common law jurisdictions of America and Australia one finds illustrations of considerable judicial intervention. Case-management can only be taken so far if the parties are not to be alienated from this process of dispute resolution; parties must retain some influence over litigation procedures otherwise their faith in such systems will diminish. In such circumstances one can expect them to seek other forms of dispute resolution which allow them greater control (see Cairns 1994:70).

The increasing importance and acceptance of formalised case-management into court systems inevitably increases a judge's discretionary role within civil justice. Discretion naturally entails flexibility but if justice is to have a measure of consistency judicial discretion requires to be structured and to operate within certain constraining confines. Integral to a fair discretionary system will be a knowledgeable and trained judiciary. Judges will require to be mutually aware of the approach of their colleagues and the range of appropriate responses in a given situation. Though Woolf believes that inconsistency can be corrected by training, Professor Zander takes a different view believing 'inconsistency stems from legitimate differences in philosophy as to how a judge should go about the business of judging' (1996:1590). Whilst critical of Woolf's proposal, Zander offers no alternative. The essence is whether training will discipline minds or emancipate them; or whether judicial minds are capable of being trained.

Civil procedure has until now operated on the basis of unrestricted access to the courts by litigants. Moreover, the parties have essentially controlled the conduct of the litigation with the court adopting an almost passive role. Latterly, there has been acceptance that the courts have a right to be more proactive, overriding the parties wishes in the process on the basis of the nebulous concept of public interest (see Glasser 1993; Damaska 1986:104-140).

Failure of ossified systems of reform – no wholesale review

Lord Gill has described the current Scottish system 'a contemporary relic of a vanquished age which is ill-serving the litigant' (1995:129). He argues that 'piecemeal approach to reform, institutionalised in rules committees, standing committees, advisory committees and the like must give place to a comprehensive review of civil justice, with no assumption in favour of the status quo, in which the public would have a proper voice' (1995:219). Earlier reviews of aspects of Scottish civil procedure have failed to address the issue of wholesale review. Lord Gill whilst noting the long standing traditional approach adopted by the Scottish civil courts expresses incredulity that the system continues to endure in the modern era (1995:130). Lord Gill is not alone in calling for a review (see Mays 1997; Scolag 1996). The desire for wholesale review is borne out of dissatisfaction with fundamental aspects of the system and the lack of strategic overview. In addition to this there is concern that there is no wide involvement in the reform process and it is the suppliers who largely determine the procedural rules and that they have 'no obvious incentive to devise those rules to meet the private preferences of individual litigants' (Ogus 1996:3). If there is to be widespread public confidence in civil justice systems, it is undoubtedly time to seek broader involvement in the process of reform.

Conclusion

Recent changes and recent proposals for imminent change in traditional dispute mechanisms and the development of ADR provision in Scotland, point to a changing landscape. The approach so far has generally been reformist rather than revolutionary. This is not to minimise the significance of the changes. Traditional methods of dispute resolution – litigation and arbitration – have not been swept away in a revolutionary tide of ADR. Instead, they have shown a willingness to respond and adapt. Consensualism and consensual methods of resolving disputes are undoubtedly gathering support. They will play a large part in future dispute resolution methodology. The advent of ADR itself has proved a catalyst for reform and has added to those existing methods to form a wider menu of choices for the disputing party. In surveying this changing landscape it is perhaps time to consider dispensation of the word 'alternative' and substituting for it, the word 'appropriate'. Multi-track reformed procedural litigation systems, arbitration and mediation and strong links between all of them will ensure a civil justice system where the party can select, or be directed to, the mechanism best suited to resolution of their dispute and the one most in keeping with societal desire to provide appropriate mechanisms without placing an undue financial burden on the rest of the community. We appear to be on the way to providing varied mechanisms for dispute resolution. The challenge will be to develop and offer the optimum form in each mechanism. In that respect much work remains to be done. Litigation procedure reform would benefit from wholesale review where analysis of the broader view could be undertaken. The current piecemeal, reformist approach continues to perpetuate unnecessary vagaries and complexities. Arbitration needs to reassess its role and in the process reconsider how it fits in with the other forms of dispute resolution. ADR needs to develop and gain wider appreciation. It may need to develop standards and regulation. It will certainly need to define its relationship with the courts. As we progress to the new millennium, the work that has been done should not mask the work that requires to be done. There is nonetheless scope for reasonable optimism that many of the issues raised here can, and will, be addressed in the not too distant future. As we reflect on Professor Hamson's barometer test of society, we may yet attain a position where we can be proud of the national values enshrined in our civil dispute resolution mechanisms. For the moment we still have some way to go.

Bibliography

Adler, M. and Morris, S. (1996). Thinking about Dispute Resolution: Alternatives to ADR. Paper for Socio-Legal Studies Association Conference, April.

Anonymous. Arbitration and Judicial Review. *Scots Law Times*; 113–116.

Brown, H. and Marriot, A. (1995). *ADR Principles and Practice*. London: Sweet and Maxwell.

Cairns, B.C. (1994). Managing Civil Litigation : An Australian Adaption of American Experience. *Civil Justice Quarterly*; 50–70.

Clancy, R., Murray, A., and Wadia, R. (1997). The New Commercial Cause Rules *Scots Law Times*; 45–49 and 53–58.

Clark, B. (1996). Alternative Dispute resolution: The next step forward? *Scottish Law Gazette*, **64**; 19.

Clark, B. and Mays, R. (1997). Funding ADR in Scotland. *Scots Law Times*; 29–34.

Clark, B. and Mays, R. (1996). Regulating ADR – the Scottish Experience. *Web Journal of Legal Issues*.

Consultation Paper on Legislation for Domestic Arbitration in Scotland (1997). Scottish Advisory Committee on Arbitration Law, Chairman Lord Dervaird, Scottish Courts Administration.

Cullen, The Hon Lord (1995). *Review of Business of the Outer House of the Court of Session*.

Damaska, (1996). *The Faces of Justice and State Authority*. Yale University Press.

Davidson, F.P. (1993). *The Practice of Arbitration in Scotland 1986–1990*. Scottish Office Central Research Report.

Davidson, F.P. (1989a). The Future of the Scots Law of Arbitration. *Scots Law Times*; 213–218.

Davidson, F.P. (1989b). Stated Cases Under the Administration of Justice (Scotland) Act 1972 s3. *Scots Law Times*; 89–94.

Davidson, F. P. (1989c). The Law relating to the Operation of Arbitral Tribunals – Room for Improvement SLG 42.

Gill, Hon Lord (1995). The case for a Civil Justice Review. *Journal of the Law Society of Scotland*, **40**; 129–132.

Glasser, C. (1993). Civil Procedure and the Lawyers – the Adversary System and the Decline of the Orality Principle. *Modern Law Review*, **56**; 3.

Greatbach and Dingwall (1996). Who's in charge? Rhetoric and Evidence in the Study of Mediation. *Journal of Social and Welfare and Family Law*; 367.

Hunter, R. F. (1987). *The Law of Arbitration in Scotland*. Edinburgh: T. and T. Clark.

Kelbie, D. (1994). *Small Claims Procedure in the Sheriff Court*. Edinburgh: Butterworths.

Jaconelli, J. (1992). Solomonic Justice and the Common Law. *Oxford Journal of Law and Society*, **12**; 480–506.

Jolowicz, J.A. (1988). Comparative law and the reform of civil procedure. *Legal Studies*, **8**; 1–13.

Jolowicz, J. A. (1996). The Woolf Report and the Adversary System. *Civil Justice Quarterly*; 198–210.

Macphail, I. (1988). *Sheriff Court Practice*. SULI 1988.

Marriott, A. (1995). The politics of Arbitration. *Civil Justice Quarterly*; 125–130.

Mays, R. and Clark, B. (1997). Alternative Dispute Resolution and the Courts. *Scottish Law and Practice Quarterly*, **2**; 57–66.

Mays, R. and Clark, B. (1996). *Alternative Dispute Resolution in Scotland*. Scottish Office Central Research Unit Report, Robert Gordon University, Aberdeen.

Mays, R. (1996). Where now for the summary cause procedure? *Scottish Law and Practice Quarterly*.

Mays, R. (1998). Case Management in the Scottish Civil Courts. *Scottish Law and Practice Quarterly* (forthcoming).

Mays, R. (1997). Frying Pan, Fire or Melting Pot – Reform of Scottish Civil Justice in the 1990s. *Juridical Review*, **2**; 91–109.

Mays, R. (1995). *Summary Cause Procedure in the Sheriff Court*. Edinburgh: Butterworths.

Millar, R. (1932). Civil Pleading in Scotland *Michigan Law Review*, **30**; 545.

Moody, S. and Mackay (eds) (1995). *Green's Guide to Alternative Dispute Resolution in Scotland*. Edinburgh: W. Green/Sweet and Maxwell.

Morgan, R. (1993). An Introduction to the Law and Practice of Arbitration in Scotland. *Arbitration*, February; 24–28.

Morris, S. and Headrick, D. (1995). *Pilgrims Process? Defended actions in the Sheriff's Ordinary Court*. Central Research Unit, Scottish Office.

Morrison, N. (1996). The Cullen Report. *Scots Law Times*; 93–100.

Murray, J. (1997). Letting Arbiters Get on With the Job. *Scots Law Times*; 64–66.

Neilson, H. S. (1993). Sheriff Court Options Hearings – Beware the Ides of March. *Journal of the Law Society*, **38**; 425–426.

Ogus, A. (1996). Some Reflections on the Woolf Interim Report Web JCLI, 1.

Raitt, F. (1995). Mediation as a form of Alternative Dispute Resolution: a rejoinder. *Journal of the Law Society of Scotland*, **40**; 182.

Renfrew, Hon C. B. (1997). The American Experience with Dispute resolution in all its forms. *Civil Justice Quarterly*, **16**; 45–155.

Schwarzer, W. (1996). Case Management in Federal Courts. *Civil Justice Quarterly*; 141–147.

Schwarzer, W. and Hirsch, A. (1991). *The Elements of Case Management*. Federal Judicial Center, USA.

SCOLAG (1996). A new landscape for English Civil Justice. *SCOLAG Journal* August; 116–117.

Semple, W. G. (1991). New Scottish Arbitration rules. *Arbitration*; 79–80.

Strathdee, I. (1996). Scottish construction industry arbitration procedures. *The Arbitration and Dispute Resolution Law Journal*; 24–31.

Upton, M. (1996). The Cullen Review – Reform of Procedure in the Court of Session. *Journal of the Law Society of Scotland*, **41**, 3; 87–117.

Wertheimer, A. (1988). The Equalization of Legal Resources. *Philosophy and Public Affairs*, **17**, 4; 303–322.

Woolf, The Right Hon Lord (1995). *Access to Justice* – interim report to the Lord Chancellor on the civil justice system in England and Wales.

Zander, M. (1996). Consistency in the Exercise of discretionary powers. *New Law Journal*, 1590.

Zuckerman, A.A.S. (1995). A reform of Civil Procedure – rationing Procedure rather than Access to Justice. *Journal of Law and Society*, **22**, 2; 155–188.

Zuckerman, A.A.S. and Cranston, R. (1995). *Reform of Civil Procedure – Essays on 'Access to Justice'*. Oxford University Press.

Fair Notice – The Role of Written Pleadings in the Civil Justice System

Andrew Murray

Introduction

Although the Scottish system of written pleading has not been without its critics in the past (see for example the comments of Lord Diplock in *Gibson v B.I.C.C.* 1973 SC (HL) 15 at 27) it has never been without its champions. There have always been those ready to defend the system from attack actual (Lord Kilbrandon in *Gibson* at p.32; Morrison 1996), or potential (Brodie 1993; Faculty of Advocates 1995). Debate on the role, and practice, of written pleading has recurred throughout the development of our system of civil litigation (see Gill 1995; Morrison 1996).

The most recent debate has been a prolonged one, its origins being in the statement of Lord Diplock in *Gibson* in 1973. Even the strongest supporters of the Scottish system of written pleadings were forced to admit pleading before the Sheriff Court required attention (Black 1982). This led to changes in the structure of civil litigation in the Sheriff Court (Ordinary Cause Rules 1993). Following amendment of the Ordinary Cause Rules, those disaffected with the state of written pleadings turned their attention to the Court of Session (see e.g. Gill 1995). Their campaign persuaded Lord President Hope to order an inquiry into Outer House procedure. Such success was not unusual for pro-reform campaigners; previous inquiries had taken place in 1834 (First Report of the Commission), 1869 (Second Report of the Commission), 1870 (Third and Fourth Reports of the Commission) and 1927 (Royal Commission on the Court of Session). The Cullen Report of 1995 stands alone among these reviews. It is the only one to recommend substantial change to our system of written pleading.

The role of written pleadings

> The purpose of the pleadings is to put clearly and shortly before the opposite Party and the Court what the pursuer's demands are – what are the questions of fact as to which the parties are in controversy, and the grounds in law on which each contends that his position is the right one.
> (Scott Dickson 1897:14)

From this statement two main functions of written pleadings may be extracted:
1. They define the issues in dispute.
2. They provide 'fair notice' of the issues.
(see Faculty of Advocates 1995).

These functions should be kept in mind when discussing any proposed changes to procedure. The role of pleadings should provide the yardstick against which any proposed changes are measured.

The first major function is to define the issues in dispute. Narrowing the issues allows parties to make the most efficient use of resources at their disposal. Well drafted written pleadings clearly set out the position of both parties and contain within a single document, the record, a transparent account of the issues in dispute. In doing so our written pleadings system allows parties, and the court, 'to ascertain and demonstrate, with precision, the matters on which the parties differ and those on which they agree; and thus to arrive at certain clear issues on which both parties require a judicial decision' (MacPhail 1988:9–03). This provides tangible benefits to the parties and the court. The parties benefit as they do not waste time and money investigating issues not in dispute. This should lead to cheaper and faster determination of their case. The court benefits as there are limited judicial resources available for allocation to civil duties (Maxwell 1986). By forcing the parties to consider their own case the points in issue are substantially reduced. This allows for the most efficient use of the judicial resource.

The doctrine of 'fair notice' provides all the benefits discussed above and more. Fair notice ensures that justice may be found in our civil justice system in more than name alone. All too commonly fair notice is misunderstood as meaning fair notice to one's opponent only. Although this is a vital role of pleadings, there is the added requirement of fair notice to the court. Fair notice should ensure that neither the court nor one's opponent is taken by surprise on the day of the proof. This is a basic requirement for the provision of justice in an adversarial system. If one's opponent were in a position to 'litigate by ambush' the pursuit of justice would be in danger of being lost amongst an environment of distrust and deception.

The doctrine of fair notice, or an equivalent, is a prerequisite for an adversarial system. Without it, it becomes almost impossible to ensure justice is being done. Our system provides that the determination of the parties' dispute is exclusively based upon information supplied by them. A lack of fair notice would mean the court would be required to base its decision upon incomplete and poorly prepared material. This is to the disadvantage of the pursuit of justice. It would in most situations favour the pursuer over the defender and could lead to the development of a system where precedent is devalued. If we propose to continue with our current adversarial culture, as we apparently are (Cullen 1995:6.15), it is suggested that the doctrine of fair notice should be central to our thoughts.

The mechanics of written pleading in the Court of Session

For those unfamiliar with the Scottish system of pleading this section will acquaint you with the system of full pleading currently in use in the Court of Session, and with some more innovative systems of pleading which have been recently implemented.

To meet the requirement of fair notice the Scottish civil justice system requires parties to plead their case 'on record'. When a case comes to proof the parties may only lead evidence to establish the facts they have set out in their pleadings. This allows all parties, including the court, to map the boundaries of the case from one document. The Scottish system was not always this way. At one time the system of written pleading was complex, lengthy and required several documents to be read to make sense of the claim and defence.

The current system of written pleadings was first set out in the Court of Session Act 1825. Prior to this Act, the Scottish system of civil litigation had been the subject of a debate not unlike the one we find ourselves with today (Morrison 1996:94). Complaints had been recorded on the slow progress of actions, the cause of which was said to be the system of written pleading. The system in place of initial pleadings, condescendences (written statements of the alleged facts forming the basis of the claim) and memorials (written statements of the legal principles founded upon) led to written pleadings of considerable length and complexity which served only to obfuscate and delay. This was unsatisfactory, and in place of these many lengthy and complex documents two replacements were introduced. These were the summons (or petition) and defences. These documents still form the basis of actions in the Court of Session, and the current rules regulating their form and application are found in the Rules of the Court of Session 1994 (RCS).

The Summons

The summons is the usual method by which actions are raised in the Court of Session. The rules prescribe the form a summons must take (RCS13.2): this includes, 'a statement, in the form of numbered articles of the condescendence, of the averments of fact which form the grounds of the claim' (RCS 13.2(3)(a)). It is in the condescendence that the pursuer sets out the facts upon which he is basing his case. These facts must, along with his pleas-in-law which also form part of his summons, demonstrate to the court that he has an arguable case for the court to hear. If he fails to make out a *prima facia* case in his summons it will be ruled irrelevant and the court will not hear his case.

The condescendence forms the heart of the pursuer's case. This is the factual basis of his action. It is here that the defender and the court are given 'fair notice' of the case the pursuer intends to prove. As has been said, according to the Scottish system the parties are unable to plead issues not on record. Thus when the defender receives the summons he may immediately begin preparing his defence in the knowledge that he may restrict his preparation to meeting those issues raised in the summons. This should allow the defender to prepare his case without wasting resources on issues which are not in dispute. The court should then have the best information available to it when the case comes to proof, both parties having focused their efforts on the pertinent issues.

The Defences

The defender is then allowed to answer the pursuer's claim by entering into record their defences. By RCS 18.1(1)(a) defences consist of: 'numbered answers corresponding to the articles of the condescendence annexed to the summons'.

Looking at the role of written pleadings it is clear that defences fulfil both the main functions of pleadings. They give the pursuer and the court 'fair notice' of the defender's case and they start the process of defining (and narrowing) the issues in dispute between the parties.

The Scottish system of summons and defences is remarkably efficient in narrowing the issues in dispute. There are several reasons for this, not least of which is the fact that the pursuer's claims are met with direct responses of admitted, denied or not known, and these responses are set beside the pursuer's claims in the open record. This allows parties to rapidly narrow the issues in dispute between them, often leading to settlement of the dispute without involving the court.

Late settlement is sometimes seen as a problem by the courts (Cullen 1995:3.38–3.41). Although late settlement is undoubtedly inconvenient for those who have made arrangements for the hearing, and for witnesses who may have travelled to give evidence, it is hard to believe that late settlement is the main cause of delay in the disposal of actions as was represented to Lord Cullen (Cullen 1995:3.39). Such a statement implies that if preparation has been made it is the duty of the parties to proceed to full hearing. This cannot be so. The litigation is the litigation of the parties. It does not become the property of the courts when an action is raised. The courts are there to facilitate the disposal of the issues in dispute. If this is achieved by settlement **at any stage** the courts have carried out their function. Lord Cullen found that 94.3% of cases in his survey settled. This suggests that the narrowing of issues, which begins with the lodging of defences, helps parties find common ground without recourse to judicial involvement in almost 19 out of 20 cases.

Adjustment and Amendment

Following the lodging of defences a period of adjustment is provided. This is an eight week period during which either party may adjust their pleadings on record (RCS 22.2). This period is to allow parties to refine their pleadings, taking account of their opponent's statements of fact and law, and to incorporate any new information which may have come to light. At this point parties narrow the issues in dispute. When the open record is made up each becomes fully aware of the other's case allowing them to carry out a focused investigation of the alleged facts. This leads to fresh admissions and further clarification of the issues in dispute.

It is possible to present a motion to the court allowing for a continuation of the adjustment period. In practice it is usually relatively easy to get a single eight week extension but after that the court looks closely at applications and it is more difficult to convince the judge to keep the record open past sixteen weeks for adjustment (Lord Cullen found the average extension granted was only 8.5 weeks Cullen 1995:3.9). Thus, on average, cases have sixteen weeks for adjustment.

Amendment is the process of altering one's pleadings once the record has been closed. Once the record has been closed the parties should be ready to go to proof on the record as it stands. This does not mean our system should be so inflexible as to prevent parties from making changes to their pleadings following closure of the record. The procedure to allow amendment is contained in RCS Ch.21. Unlike adjustment, amendment is controlled by the court. There needs to be an application to amend and the court must grant its permission. This provides the best solution when balancing the functions of pleadings. It allows for further definition of the issues in dispute, while at the same time allowing the court to ensure that all parties have fair notice of the issues. Critics of amendment should remember that the action is the parties' action, not the court's. If amendment is needed to focus the issues then the parties should be allowed to amend provided they do not risk the interests of justice in so doing.

At the end of the amendment process the parties may elect to go to proof of the facts in dispute or to debate on the legal issues. Either of those hearings is based upon the issues on record. This allows the parties and the presiding judge to prepare a framework for the hearing while working from a single document.

Specialised procedures in the Court of Session

Although the procedure described above is the ordinary procedure for actions in the Court of Session there are some specialised procedures which make use of abbreviated pleading.

The first of these procedures is the optional procedure for personal injury actions (RCS 43.18). This expressly provides for brief statements of fact in the condescendence followed by brief answers from the defender. There is no automatic period of adjustment. Parties wishing to adjust/amend must show special cause (RCS 43.24(5)(a)&(b)). The optional procedure has slightly more judicial pro-activity than the ordinary procedure, for instance at the Diet Roll hearing, which takes place after defences have been lodged, the judge can order further specification of the pleadings.

The optional procedure is designed to meet a specific type of action. It is to provide inexpensive and expeditious access to a judge in simple cases. It is designed specifically for those personal injury cases where the issues are clear and no amount of detailed pleading will narrow the issues between the parties.

> The optional procedure appears to be ideally suited to cases arising out of road traffic accidents and to cases arising out of industrial accidents where the facts are in a relatively small compass and the medical evidence is straightforward. It does not, however, follow that the procedure is appropriate to all actions in which more complex issues are raised.
> (Lord Jauncey in Giles v Fleming Bros. 1987 SLT 114 at 115).

Abbreviated pleadings are also in use in the Court of Session for actions raised under the commercial cause rules (RCS c.47). As with the optional cause procedure parties are expected to make short statements of facts and there is no automatic period for adjustment. Unlike the optional procedure this is not a procedure designed to deal with simple cases that may be dealt with quickly and cheaply. Instead the commercial roll represents the 'Rolls-Royce' of Court of Session procedures. Once defences have been entered parties are allocated to a commercial judge for a preliminary hearing. At this stage the issues in dispute are narrowed and clarified. Instead of parties being left to their own devices to provide clarification of the issues there is continual guidance from the commercial judge at continued preliminary hearings which may take place over several weeks or months. On the commercial roll there is judicially controlled and monitored adjustment of the pleadings.

These are the current models of written pleading used in the Court of Session. Following his inquiry, Lord Cullen suggested that the ordinary procedure be replaced for the bulk of ordinary actions by a procedure similar to that in the optional procedure for personal injury: was he right to do so?

The proposals for change

Despite evidence that the Scottish system of full pleading is one of the best available to meet the stated purposes of written pleading it has some vocal critics who feel it is antiquated, unduly formalistic and the cause of expense and delay.

Foremost amongst those critics is one of Scotland's most respected legal practitioners, Lord Gill. In the address to the Annual Conference of the Law Society of Scotland in 1995, Lord Gill attacked Scottish complacency suggesting a wide-scale review of our civil justice system was required, mirroring that taking place south of the border under the chairmanship of Lord Woolf. His comments on the state of written pleadings were damning:

> [E]xperience of modern practice shows us that it (current procedure) is time-consuming. It is not cost-effective. It has had its day. As to the form of pleadings, what can justify the baroque formularies which are still characteristic of grounds of fault, prayers of petitions, wills of summonses, and the like? As to substance, why have Lord Diplock's words in Gibson v BICC gone unheeded? As we enter a new millennium, do we still wish the difference between success and failure in a civil action to depend on textual criticism of the kind which cases such as Gibson exemplify?
> (Gill 1995:132).

Statements such as this, which reflected the opinion of many members of the profession (see Mays 1997; Woolman 1996), convinced Lord President Hope an inquiry into Court of Session procedure was long overdue. On 24 May 1995,

only 67 days after Lord Gill's address, Lord Hope appointed Lord Cullen to carry out a review of the business of the Outer House. One of the specific instructions of his remit was to consider the practice of pleadings. This he did, making recommendations which if implemented would lead to the single greatest change to the Scottish system of pleading for 170 years.
Lord Cullen's proposed changes are as follows:

1. All actions are to be raised by a system of abbreviated pleadings. Any action unsuitable for abbreviated pleadings can only be put to full pleading with the permission of the court following the raising of a motion to transfer (Cullen 1995:4.8).
2. The condescendence to follow the style of that used in the optional procedure for personal injury (Cullen 1995:4.9).
3. The defences are not to explicitly answer the pursuer's claims, rather they are to contain brief averments of the facts the defender intends to rely upon in resisting the action (Cullen 1995:4.14).
4. An 'extended' 21 day period for the lodging of defences (Cullen 1995:4.24). This is extended from the current 7 days following calling of the action.
5. A shortened 4 week adjustment period **for the pursuer alone**. The defender to have no absolute right to adjust without the consent of the other party or the court (Cullen 1995:4.28).

Other proposals which effect the practice of written pleadings include: abolition of the open record (4.34), judicial proactivity in the process of amendment (4.35), the introduction of a case management hearing (6.31) and the introduction of the proactive Outer House judge who is the manager of the case through a new case management system (Ch.6).

These proposals suggest a system of written pleading which would function similarly to that currently in use in the optional procedure for personal injury actions. Indeed, Lord Cullen alludes to such similarity when at para. 4.6 he says, 'At present abbreviated pleadings are competent only for the optional procedure which is available in a limited type of action. In my view such pleadings should apply in **all** types of action provided that they are appropriate to the particular case.'

There is a basic problem with such a proposal. As has already been stated the optional procedure is designed for simple personal injury cases which would not benefit from further, more detailed, pleading (see Lord Jauncey in *Giles v Fleming Bros* (supra), *Paterson v Henry Robb* (1989) SC 64, *Glennie v Gillies* (1988) SC 73). To extend a principle which was developed for factually and legally simple cases to all Outer House cases is disconcerting. It was recognised by Lord Cullen that some cases would still require full pleadings for clarification and narrowing of issues, and to this end he suggests abbreviated pleadings are used only where 'they are appropriate', and he allows for transfer to what he calls the 'extended adjustment roll' (4.16–4.17).

Lord Cullen's proposal is that all actions begin on the ordinary roll, for which the preparation of abbreviated pleadings would be required. If upon an application by either party the court finds the case to be one of 'difficulty or complexity' it will be transferred to the extended adjustment roll whereupon parties can begin to prepare full pleadings. Such a system means that in these complex cases the preparation of pleadings will be delayed pending the outcome of the motion to transfer. Further, the costs of preparing such a motion will be borne by the parties. This would appear to add to both delay and costs, the twin targets of His Lordship's inquiry. If only a small number of cases were to be affected in this way this would not be a problem. The increased efficiency which would benefit most cases would more than compensate for the relatively minor delay and expense which would be faced by parties in complex cases. Lord Cullen, wisely, did not attempt to estimate how many cases would be benefited by his new abbreviated pleadings. He said, '[t]here are, in my view, many cases in which there is no need for more than abbreviated pleadings and in which the use of traditional pleadings and the procedure associated with them is productive of delay and expense' (Cullen 1995:4.6). This has obviously not been the subject of investigation by the inquiry team, it is merely the view of Lord Cullen. Given that cases which require full pleadings face possible delay and increased cost, we must question this view.

The abbreviated pleading system used for the optional procedure in personal injury has been found insufficient to be able to deal with cases of industrial deafness (*Giles*) and asbestosis (*Paterson; Glennie*). Issues of causation make such cases too complex for the optional procedure (Smith 1997:2–3). It is designed only to deal with the simplest of cases. Lord Cullen believes that **many** cases may benefit from the expansion of the optional procedure system of pleading. If this is correct there is a more fundamental problem than those of delay and cost to be addressed. We are discussing here procedures for the Court of Session, the supreme civil court in Scotland. If it is the case that many of the actions being raised in this court are so simple that they do not even require full pleadings to narrow the issues then we must ask ourselves what purpose the Court of Session serves as a court of first instance. It would appear to be an irrational use of resources to have the country's finest legal minds engaged on such mundane matters. It would be more efficient, and certainly cheaper, to take such actions to the Sheriff Court, leaving the Court of Session to deal with appeals and Lord Cullen's 'complex cases'. It is the author's opinion that this is not the type of work Senators of the College of Justice are engaged in, but if it is it indicates there are considerable problems with our system of civil litigation.

Lord Cullen's statement may not, though, be so simply deconstructed. His statement at para.4.6, needs to be read in light of the remainder of his report, and particularly Chapter 6. At this point in his report, Lord Cullen advocates the introduction of case management in the Outer House (6.15). He advocates a system of 'loose' case management where parties are to appear before the court at certain 'milestone' dates. In the proposed system for the Outer House two milestone dates are prescribed, these are:

1. The case management hearing – to take place at the end of the adjustment period, and

2. Pre-proof reviews – to take place before proof or jury trial.

From our point of view the more interesting of these is the case management hearing. An analogy may be drawn between the case management hearing and the current preliminary hearing used in commercial actions. The judge at the case management hearing will have similar powers to those of the commercial judges (Cullen 1995 6.36–6.37;RCS 47.11). The power to focus the issues, and to decide the best procedure for the case will lie with the pro-active judge.

It is at this point that the value of Lord Cullen's proposals for abbreviated pleadings may be seen. If the judge is to be in a position to narrow the issues and to control the procedure it negates the need for the parties to prepare full pleadings. The procedure would not in fact mirror that of the optional procedure for personal injury, it would be much closer to that of the commercial cause rules. Judges will be able to deal with much more complex issues without the need for parties to flesh out pleadings. Unlike the optional procedure the commercial cause rules were not developed to deal with only simple cases, they were designed to deal with complex issues. An adoption of a procedure akin to the commercial cause procedure would allow a substantial amount of Court of Session actions to be dealt with under abbreviated pleadings. Such a process would possibly allow the 'many cases' Lord Cullen talks about to be dealt with without recourse to the extended adjustment roll.

In light of this argument, in the next section of this chapter where the effectiveness of abbreviated pleadings are evaluated, there will be an evaluation on the basis of 'simple' pleading such as those used in the optional procedure, and 'directed' pleading such as those used on the commercial roll.

Abbreviated pleadings

Abbreviated pleadings would bring benefits to our system. Stephen Woolman has discussed some of those benefits while examining the problems of the current system (Woolman 1996).

I agree with two of Mr. Woolman's three criticisms of our current system. Our system of pleading is too rigid. It does not have the inbuilt flexibility which is associated with the pursuit of justice. How can one ensure justice is being done when the system is so inflexible? The answer to that question is, of course, that we can never ensure an entirely just system. We have chosen to develop our system of civil justice as an adversarial system. We rely upon the theory that, 'the fairest decision is reached when two men argue, as unfairly as possible, on opposite sides for then it is certain that no important consideration will altogether escape notice' (Macauley quoted in Woolman 1996) For this theorem to function effectively both parties require full and complete notice of the case they are to meet, thus the requirement of inflexibility is necessary or justice may not be done. To introduce greater flexibility we need a more inquisitorial system; an evaluation of such a directed pleadings system is given below.

I also agree with Mr. Woolman's third criticism of our system. The language used in pleadings is archaic and unnecessarily complex. Pleadings should be easily understood by the parties, they are after all their pleadings prepared by counsel on their behalf. I would support a modernisation of language. This does not though have to mean that the traditional method of direct response to your opponents pleading needs to be replaced by abbreviated statements of fact from each party. Modern language and traditional pleadings could be married satisfactorily. Practitioners can explain to a client the meanings of '*brevitatis causa*' (in few words) or '*quoad ultra*' (regarding other matters), why not use the modern terms?

I find myself unable to agree with Mr. Woolman's second criticism though. He suggests that too much time is occupied by parties tinkering with their pleadings right up to the last minute. This is no doubt factually correct, and it can lead to lengthy and confusing closed records. The 'tinkering' he describes though is a function of the pleadings process. It is this which narrows the issues in dispute. Admittedly there is a problem with the management of this process, and I agree the rules should be more stringently enforced. A problem with the practice does not mean we should ignore the theory. The theory of our adjustment process is sound, and I believe that a more stringent enforcement regime would improve the practice.

An evaluation of 'simple' abbreviated pleadings

The use of simple abbreviated pleadings would indicate a system of pleading similar to that used for the optional procedure for personal injury (discussed above). In light of the earlier discussion of the role of the optional procedure, it should be considered that complex issues could not be dealt with by such a system. This would mean most cases proceeding by way of the extended adjustment roll and full pleadings. The proposed system of abbreviated pleading has, though, even greater difficulties if there is to be no judicial management of pleading.

The primary difficulty of the proposed procedure is the time limits involved. Once the inducia (the minimum period of notice between intimation of the claim, and the calling of the case in the court) has elapsed the case will no longer call, rather the defender has 21 days to lodge defences (Cullen 1995:4.24). This is then followed by a four week adjustment period **for the pursuer to adjust** (Cullen 1995:4.28). These time periods seem impractical for all but the simplest of actions. Problematic cases such as those raised to beat time-bar or those containing skeleton defences would require further definition of the pleadings. This could not simply be done on the adjustment roll, it would require either the agreement of all other parties to the action or the permission of the court (Cullen 1995:4.28). If the defender is genuinely surprised to receive the summons, 21 days will be insufficient to allow his representatives to investigate the claim and prepare full defences. Skeleton defences would, in all likelihood, be entered and would require to be fleshed out. With no automatic adjustment period in which to do this defenders will need to turn to the court to seek amendment. Judges will be forced to allow such amendment 'in the interests of justice' and the action will be delayed for amendment to take place. This will also add to costs as defenders have to prepare a motion for amendment to allow them to carry out what would traditionally have been done on the adjustment roll. In the author's opinion situations such as the one described would not be uncommon.

To remedy the problems of short preparation times, skeleton pleadings and the fact that the new abbreviated pleadings will only be short statements of fact, there would need to be greater emphasis on extraneous evidence. I would caution against using documentary evidence as an alternative to written pleadings. Currently all parties to the action can prepare for hearings on the basis of a single document. Although extraneous documentary evidence is used to supplement the pleadings, the entirety of the action can be mapped out from the four corners of a single document. If it were to prove impossible to map out the action from abbreviated (and perhaps skeletal) pleadings recourse would need to be made to extrinsic evidence. This would increase the workload of the judiciary and representatives indicating a subsequent increase in costs. Further, this may introduce to Scotland the problem of discovery which has so beset the English legal system. With greater reliance on documentary evidence, parties would require full disclosure at the earliest opportunity and the possibility of a Scottish system of discovery arising would be strong. (For a discussion of discovery see Jacob 1987:92–102). The problem with a system of discovery is that representatives are unsure which documents are directly relevant and which are not. Generally all documents will be copied 'just in case' at extra expense and then each needs to be examined in light of the (abbreviated) pleadings.

The English experience of discovery has not been good. In their representation to the Woolf inquiry, the English Bar said of discovery:

> [A]n overgenerous approach to discovery can be as disadvantageous to the outcome of a trial as a failure to give proper discovery. Not to weed out inessential documents can add to the costs at every stage of proceedings... In addition, the length of trial increases because time is spent in dealing with the paper mountain and time and cross-examination on peripheral issues is greater.
> (Woolf 1995:165)

This was echoed by the City of London Law Society who said:

> One of the major factors responsible for long delays and significant expense is the current procedural system of discovery of documents. In major commercial litigation in particular, discovery can be a huge task and the resources required to be deployed in carrying through are often the single most costly item for which the litigant will have to pay in bringing his case to trial.
> (Woolf 1995:164)

Lord Woolf came to the conclusion that discovery could only be retained if greater control over the scale of discovery was exercised (Woolf 1995:167). To achieve this control Lord Woolf suggested control of discovery was to be exercised by procedural judges, who are to be the case-managers of the new English procedure. Given the English experience if we are to implement simple abbreviated pleadings in our system control over the disclosure of information would need to be exercised. This would need to be in the hands of the judge, and would in effect see us moving closer to the theories of 'directed pleadings'. For this reason I suggest the arguments relating to the evaluation of directed abbreviated pleadings in the next section are equally applicable to evaluation of the judge as 'manager of disclosure'.

An evaluation of 'directed' abbreviated pleadings

Judicial proactivity is the focus of investigation elsewhere within this paper (see Wadia). With this in mind I will curtail my comments on the possible introduction of judicial case-management to the role it would play in the development of 'directed' pleadings.

The system of case-management proposed by Lord Cullen is that of loose or milestone case-management. The milestone which would have the greatest impact on the development of written pleadings is the proposed case-management hearing.

It has been suggested, above, that an analogy may be drawn between the proposed pre-proof review and the current preliminary hearing system used on the commercial roll. As one cannot be sure how the development of pleadings would be managed at the proposed case-management hearing I intend to make use of this analogy.

There has, to date, been a single study of the new commercial roll (Clancy et al. 1997). It has, though, given valuable insight into the role of the commercial judge.

> The court takes a hands-on approach to the identification and definition of the real issued...[i]t is rare for cases to proceed on the footing that parties are simply left to adjust their pleadings with no judicial input in the process by which facts are ascertained and presented. The court supervises the way in which pleadings develop. The supervision may involve direct impact on the content of written pleadings. The court has on occasion ordered parties to adjust pleadings on matters specified.
> (Clancy et al. 1997:53).

Given that the proposed powers listed for the judicial case-manager at the proposed case-management hearing are similar to those currently exercised by the commercial judges at preliminary hearings (Cullen 1995:6.36–6.39: RCS 47.11) it is reasonable to assume the judicial case-managers would be required to regulate issues in dispute in a similar manner.

This would indicate a radical shift away from the traditional role of written pleadings. Instead of the parties (and representatives) narrowing the issues in dispute, responsibility for this task would now lie with the judicial case-manager. Although such a shift of responsibility would undoubtedly deal with Lord Cullen's five criticisms of the current practice of pleading (discussed intra, p.62), judicial proactivity is not the best solution.

There is no doubt that judicial proactivity has been successful in the rarefied atmosphere of the commercial roll, but the commercial roll should be seen as a one-off. The commercial roll was introduced to meet the problems that were being caused by excessive delays on the ordinary roll. It was perceived that commercial organisations may take their business elsewhere if a procedure was not developed to provide a speedy and controlled resolution to their problems (Coulsfield 1993). The success of the commercial roll in achieving these aims is without question (Clancy et al. 1997), but we must ask ourselves if it is possible to even consider providing such a service for all actions in the Outer House. As part of the team who studied the commercial roll, the author's opinion is that such a procedure is unsuitable for all Outer House actions.

Firstly, although the new commercial roll was designed to meet claims of undue expense, the amount of 'hands-on' judicial involvement means extra expense at the pre-proof stage of an action. There is greater front loading of costs to allow representatives to answer pertinent questions at the preliminary hearing stage. A high level of preparation is required for the initial preliminary hearing which will be within 14 days of lodging defences (RCS 47.8(2)).

Secondly, only the hardiest of counsel will be willing to oppose the commercial judge at such a hearing. This means, in effect, the judge narrows the issues in dispute and decides the course of action to be taken (admittedly from information supplied by counsel). This is not to be encouraged. The usual method of pleading allows the parties and their representatives to narrow the issues. This is as it should be. It is the parties who have first hand knowledge of the issues in dispute. It is bad enough that pleadings are drafted by advocates who have been instructed by solicitors, who in turn have been instructed by the client. This means pleadings are drafted based on third hand information. Allowing the judge to set the agenda means fourth hand information is being used, and as clients rarely attend hearings the accuracy of such information cannot be verified.

The third and final reason why case-management cannot currently be used in this way is the time constraints involved in hearing an action. Currently the commercial judges allow half an hour for each preliminary hearing. Almost every case raised receives at least one preliminary hearing for which the judge has to read the papers. Each full-time commercial judge can hear six or more preliminary/procedural hearings on any Monday. When the last full-scale review of the use of judicial time in the Court of Session was undertaken it was found that on average judges worked an extra seven hours per week over their allocated time for judicial duties (Maxwell 1986:5.15). The position today is, if anything, worse in this respect.

Our system only functions due to teamwork between the bench, the bar and the administration. Part of that teamwork is the requirement that members of the bar narrow the issues in dispute. Once the issues have been narrowed 95% of cases settle. With members of the judiciary already overworked we cannot justify a case-management hearing for these cases. By allowing each case a half-hour case-management hearing to discuss the issues the workload of all Outer House judges would be increased out of proportion with the prospective benefits which may accrue from such hearings. Without a considerable increase in court resources such an increase in judicial workload could not be met. As such a cash injection is unlikely from a new government which has pledged to keep a tight control on public spending I suggest that directed pleadings are not the solution to Lord Cullen's criticisms of current practice.

The future role of pleadings

From the results of this evaluation of abbreviated written pleadings it would appear there is no discernible advantage to their implementation; further, there is no evidence to suggest that they would provide a better system for the provision of fair notice or for the narrowing of the issues in dispute. It is therefore to be respectfully suggested that Lord Cullen's proposals are not the best available for actions in the Outer House and that further options for the refinement of written pleadings should be investigated.

Lord Cullen identified five criticisms of the current practice of written pleadings:

1. over-elaboration of details,
2. lack of candour in defences,
3. undue reliance on points of pleading,
4. the system is unduly elaborate, and
5. a failure to give notice to the courts.

The task we must set ourselves is how best to deal with these (valid) criticisms if we are not to adopt the approach advocated by Lord Cullen.

Firstly, it must be accepted that some form of written pleading is necessary to allow for the functioning of the adversarial system which we operate. From this point it is clear that if we are to reject proposals for abbreviated pleadings we must retain the current system of full pleading. This conclusion is, happily, in line with the majority of opinions expressed to the author in a limited survey which was conducted prior to the preparation of this paper. In addition, it needs to be accepted that the current system is in need of development to allow for the expeditious and efficient disposal of actions. The problems identified by Lord Cullen need a solution. This is not in dispute. All that is being suggested here is that the solution offered by Lord Cullen may not be the best available. Before we sacrifice hundreds of years of steady development we should attempt to find a solution which would allow us the benefits of full pleading while dealing with the problems identified by Lord Cullen. It is my suggestion that the solution may lie with the standards the Scottish legal profession is required to meet.

Professional responsibility

> Each one of us has a reason for following 'good practice' for the good of the profession as a whole because we depend for our livelihood on public support and confidence in all members of the profession.
> (Webster and Webster 1996:1)

This statement offers a solution to those criticisms currently levelled at our system of written pleading. If it is true that the current state of written pleadings is such that they are over-elaborate and lack candour, this must be seen as a reflection of the profession. If we do nothing to remedy this we shall all suffer the consequences in the long-term. All members of the profession are officers of the court. This means that they have many duties to the court which transcend personal interests and the interests of their client.

> Every counsel... [a]s an officer of the court concerned in the administration of justice, has an overriding duty to the court, to the standards of his profession and to the public.
> (Lord Reid in *Rondel v Worsley* [1967] 3 All ER 993 at 998F).

It is the opinion of the author that although counsel certainly support the above statement, and would if asked say that they carry out their duty to the court with diligence, the factual position currently is that in the preparation of pleadings only lip-service is paid to the duty. A glance through any set of pleadings makes it abundantly clear where counsel (and solicitors) have failed in their duty to the court. Skeleton defences are not uncommon, nor are pleadings which lack clarity and candour. All too often adjustment comes in a flurry during the last few days on the adjustment roll, showing that the case has been shelved while other matters were being dealt with, only coming to the fore as the deadline loomed. This, to paraphrase Lord Reid, shows a lack of concern for the administration of justice, and it is this which is the key to solving the problems of our system.

It is, of course, a fact of life in the legal profession today that people are taking on more work for less reward. Increased competition in both branches of the profession mean that practitioners push themselves to the limit. This has led to greater use of modern technology in an attempt to increase efficiency (not a new phenomenon see Dundas 1903:332) . Practitioners regularly use 'that agency of the devil' (Black 1982:17) the dictating machine, and today there is an increased use of the word processor with inbuilt templates: 'fill in the blanks pleading'. This leads to what Professor Black has labelled 'stream of consciousness pleading' (Black 1982:17). The pleader due to pressures of work misses out step one in the preparation of pleadings: having the issues clear in his mind (Dundas 1903:329; Black 1982:3).

There is no easy answer to this problem, but the profession must realise that if it does not face the problem of badly drafted pleadings now, it will only become a greater problem. To this end I suggest that members of the profession take greater responsibility for the drafting and adjustment of pleadings.

Currently an advocate or a solicitor acting as an advocate cannot be sued for any negligent act *bona fide* done or omitted to be done by him while conducting a case in court (*Batchelor v Pattison & Mackersy* (1876) 3R 914). This immunity extends to the preparation of pleadings. The immunity is based on logical foundations. The advocate's duty to the court cannot be compromised by his duty to the client, and to allow the client a suit of action may so compromise this duty. Further, the advocate must be independent to conduct the case according to his own judgement. To allow the client a challenge to the actions of counsel would damage such independence.

The law today is less clear cut than it was in 1876. The House of Lords has stated that counsel's immunity is the exception rather than the rule. It has been further stated that Barristers owe a general duty of care to their clients (*Saif Ali v Sydney Mitchell & Co.* [1980] AC 198), and that the Barristers immunity for court work arises out of reasons of public policy (*Rondel; Saif Ali*). With this in mind we must ask ourselves whether extending such immunity to cover the preparation of pleadings is in the public interest.

It is my belief that counsel should not be made responsible to their client for the preparation of written pleadings. It would be detrimental to the independence of the bar to do so. Counsel must be able to prepare the foundations of the case without fear of later litigation. I would reject any proposal to abolish the advocate's immunity during the preparation of pleadings.

I do not, though, believe that counsel should face total immunity in the preparation of written pleadings. The English legal system has led the way in accounting for the actions of legal representatives in the preparation of an action. By virtue of Ss.51(6)&(7) of the *Supreme Court Act 1981* and *Rules of the Supreme Court* Ord.62 rr.10,11&28, a court may make a wasted costs order. 'Wasted costs' are defined in s.51(7) as:

> costs incurred by a party (a) as a result of any improper, unreasonable or negligent act or omission on the part of any legal or other representative or any employee of such a representative; or (b) which, in the light of any such act or omission occurring after they were incurred, the court considers it is unreasonable to expect that party to pay.

If the court finds such negligence on the part of the legal representative then it can find the representative personally liable for the costs incurred. These orders extend to counsel as well as solicitors (*R. v Secretary of State for the Home Department ex parte Abbassi* [1992] TLR 170) and can extend to simple wasting of time by counsel (*Antonelli v Wade Gery Farr* [1992] TLR 652). There is absolutely no reason why members of the Scottish profession should not face similar court supervision in the preparation and development of written pleadings. Such supervision falls far short of case-management. The parties remain free to define and narrow the issues in dispute, but when preparing pleadings representatives will be aware that their blanket immunity has gone. Such a role for the judge should ensure that counsel are entirely candid when preparing pleadings, and should ensure clarity of pleading. Counsel will not wish to meet costs themselves. This solution should be able to meet Lord Cullen's five criticisms of the current system without the need to replace our current system of full pleading.

Conclusion

Although our current system of written pleading is not without its problems, it should be remembered that it has many more good points than bad. We must not allow ourselves to be won over by a small group of dissident voices who suggest that it can only be improved upon by abolition. Our rules of written pleading are, in the author's opinion, some of the best in the world. The unfortunate position we find ourselves in today is a reflection of the fact that they have been inadequately enforced for too long. If we provide some teeth for the judiciary we should quickly see an improvement in the standard of pleading.

Finally a plea to all those who are calling for urgent and widespread reform of the written pleadings system. We have an excellent framework here which is only in need of enforcement. We should try enforcing the rules we have before we throw out the rulebook and start over.

Bibliography

Black, R., (1982). *An introduction to written pleadings.* Law Society of Scotland.

Brodie, P.H., (1993). Basic guiding principles (of written pleadings). *Law Society of Scotland Update.* Law Society of Scotland; 6–23.

Clancy, R., Murray, A., and Wadia, R., (1997). The new commercial cause rules. *Scots Law Times (News)*; 45–49, 53–58.

Coulsfield, The Hon Lord, (1993). *Report of the review body on commercial actions in the Court of Session.* Scottish Courts Administration.

Cullen, The Hon Lord, (1995). *Review of the business of the Outer House of the Court of Session.* Scottish Courts Administration.

Dundas, D., (1903). Observations on the art of advocacy. *Juridical* Review **15**; 329–349.

Faculty of Advocates (Committee on the Courts), (1995). *Reform of the Court of Session practice.* (Internal submission to Lord Cullen's inquiry team).

Gill, The Hon Lord, (1995). The case for a civil justice review. *Journal of the Law Society of Scotland*, **40**; 129–133.

Jacob, J.I.H., (1987). *The Fabric of English Civil Justice.* Hamlyn/Stevens and Sons, London.

Jacob, J.I.H., Goldrein, I., (1990). *Pleadings, Principles and Practice.* Sweet and Maxwell, London.

Macphail, I.R., (1988). *Sheriff Court practice and procedure.* W. Green and Sons/SULI, Edinburgh.

Maxwell, The Hon Lord, (1986). *Report of the review body on the use of judicial time in the superior courts in Scotland.* Scottish Court Administration.

Mays, R., (1997). Frying pan, fire or melting pot? – reforming Scottish civil justice in the 1990s. *Juridical Review*, **42**; 91–109.

Morrison, N., (1996). The Cullen report. *Scots Law Times (News)*; 93–100.

Morrison, N., Bartos, D., Higgins, T., Maclean, I., Haldane Tait, J. and Wolffe, S., (1994). *Annotated Rules of the Court of Session.* W. Green and Sons, Edinburgh.

Scott Dickson, C., (1897). Pleading. *Juridical Review*, **9**; 14–33.

Smith, S., (1997). Running a reparation action. *Law Society of Scotland Update.* Law Society of Scotland.

Webster, J.J., and Webster R.M., (1996). *Professional Ethics and Practice for Scottish Solicitors.* T. and T. Clark, Edinburgh; 2–17.

Woolf, The Rt. Hon Lord, (1995). *Access to justice (interim report)* HMSO.

Woolman, S., (1996). Pleadings: *Scots Law into the 21st century*, MacQueen, H. (ed), W.Green/Sweet & Maxwell; 277–283.

Judicial Case Management
The Quiet but Significant Revolution[1]

Rachel Wadia

Revolution or Evolution?

> Our law cannot stand still if it is to remain an acceptable rule of conduct amid rapidly changing human relationships. It must doubtless bring original thought to bear on its new problems; but original thought can be a dangerous and dubious guide and may lead different minds to surprisingly divergent and not always equitable solutions unless it is brought to the test of fundamental principle.[2]

Lord Normand's words of wisdom in 1937 retain their potency and reflect a current dilemma within Scottish courts. The guardians of our civil justice system stand seemingly undecided on the threshold of revolutionary changes to its working practices; changes which have been part of an evolutionary process in other common law jurisdictions around the world over the last 30 years; changes which now threaten power structures and the alteration of traditional roles in a redefinition of justice; changes which may increase access to the courts and quicken the litigating process but bring their own inherent problems.

This paper highlights some of the current problems which govern the operation of our civil courts and questions whether simply drafting new procedural rules, without establishing the extent of the problems and without addressing the effects of existing working conventions, will actually benefit the client, the profession or the court. The distillation of historical and cross-jurisdictional analysis will be used to show that in Scotland we have proved the theory that judicial intervention propels cases towards resolution. The danger lies in propelling a small jurisdiction to wholesale reform without agreement on fundamental principles, cohesion and unity of purpose.

Complex and conflicting principles are involved, and together with the subjective perspectives of the court players work against consensus in a unique legal system. However problems which have been highlighted both historically in Scotland and to a greater extent in other adversarial systems are depressingly consistent – the high cost of litigation, long delays, late settlements, restricted resources, heavy criminal workloads, lack of empirical research and resistance to change. Despite previous attempts at reform aimed at addressing these problems, and calls for management of the litigation process, there is ample evidence that the court system is still run on the basis of crisis management.

The nature of the work and the fact that the litigation process is currently uncontrolled means that it is an open-ended demand-led reactive system, not a proactive service. A purist would say that this is the court's proper role, but particularly since 1979 constraints on government expenditure have gradually invaded all public service institutions (Lord Rodger of Earlsferry 1994:9), and the legal system has not been immune. Reality challenges theory. Competition from within and outwith the profession means that structural, economic and social forces are converging to prompt a fresh look at court reform at a time when case numbers are falling but costs for the client, court and public purse are rising.

The latest call for radical change in Scotland was forcefully presented by Lord Cullen's Review of the Outer House Administration in December 1995. At the heart of the Review is the proposal that management of cases should no longer rest with the parties and their representatives, but be monitored and supervised by the judges – judicial case management. This fundamental change falls directly in line with the attempts of other common law adversarial jurisdictions to provide greater access to justice while implanting a cost-effective business strategy on internal administrative procedure. The recommendations of the Review also follow the pattern of previous Scottish reform proposals on the need for judicial control. In practice reforms have failed to change the established working cultures, a barrier which has been encountered in other jurisdictions (Jacob 1986:284, Glasser 1990:7). Zuckerman also argues (1995:67) that unless a judicial system addresses the underlying conventions which shape the rules in practice, any procedural rule change will be a further waste of public and private money. Acknowledging that working attitudes underpin reforms (1995:6.26), the Cullen Review is seen as the first real challenge to the principled foundations of the legal system in Scotland.

The move towards reform is supported by a combination of the judiciary's frustration with what they see as increasingly inept practices and the more public-oriented 'Access to Justice' campaign which is creating a pincer movement towards reform. The balance and boundaries of behaviour are matters of principle reflecting both the individual integrity and culture of each country, but revolving around a common concept – an adversarial legal system – giving the parties full control of the pace, disclosure and presentation of their case. This can turn litigation into professional combat, wielding the weapons of skilled presentation and tactical brinkmanship to champion the client's cause. Today's increasingly competitive and rights-conscious society reinforces this attitude, but no other public service – for example, health or education – allows clients unfettered access or control to their procedures or resources. Is civil justice more important? It may be true that in some cases it is as much a part of a lawyer's duty to the client to delay and increase costs for the opposing party as it is to prepare a case for adjudication, but for how long can parties expect to use the full panoply of procedural options in the name of justice regardless of the value of the claim, the resources available and the numbers of litigants queuing for court time? The integrity of a judicial system is compromised by condoned practice, and leads us to question its fundamental purpose before we can address its current needs.

What is Civil Justice?

A civil justice system has been defined as 'that vast arena in which disputes of fact and law between individuals, corporate bodies and the state are resolved' (Hope 1992:7), and has been accepted for centuries as the poor relation of the criminal system which is regulated by its own tight time limits. However as the Hughes Commission on Legal Services in Scotland acknowledged, since governments have created a plethora of personal rights since the War they have a moral responsibility to facilitate the exercise of those rights and obligations (Hughes 1980:1.34). This means creating access to justice for all. The Court's role in fulfilling these obligations is to

- provide a means of peaceful and effective resolution of disputes
- publish and apply key legal, political and social values and norms
- set down a rule of law for all by precedent
- act as a channel of communication (e.g. between debtor and creditor)
- publicly recognise the worth of human rights
- provide a focus for negotiation and settlement
- introduce a greater awareness of legality in administration

The standards which a legal system should provide were defined by Lord Mackay of Clashfern as impartiality, compulsion, finality, potential for certainty – all on a cost-effective basis (1994:75). These ideals beg a list of questions. Does the Scottish legal system meet these standards and the needs of the people it serve? Do these needs actually conflict? Can we put a price and time limit on justice? Do the time and costs involved actually create an incentive to negotiate and settle? Are they in fact private bargaining tools and therefore resistant to any form of court control?

What Does the Client Want?

It is not often that this question is addressed within the legal profession. Client perception in an increasingly consumer-conscious and competitive arena is new to a monopolistic market hitherto protected by a cultural mystique. But as the Hon. Justice Zuber stated

> The principle that courts exist for the benefit of litigants and the public is one which must be kept in mind whenever reform or restructuring of the courts is under consideration. The courts are like all institutions, they tend to take on a life of their own.... the comfort of those working in the courts is not the primary goal of the reform of the court system. (Report on Ontario Courts Enquiry 1987:5.3).

At the moment, the client takes the progression of his case on trust, with no information given by the court.

In a 1995 study of over 1,000 recent litigants (National Consumer Council and B.B.C. Law in Action) only 8% stated that they wanted their case to go to a full trial, 23% would have preferred to sit around a table with an expert making the final decision, and 53% would have preferred to make the decision themselves under the same conditions (1995:26). Only 40% were seeking monetary compensation (which is what litigation is arguably geared to provide), 50% wanted to prevent recurrence of a problem, 17% an apology, 10% to apportion blame. The courts were seen as cumbersome, slow, complex and vulnerable to manipulation. Submissions to the Cullen Review, the contemporary English Woolf Report, Canadian Zuber Report, Australian Sackville Report, Federal Judicial Center and American Bar Association's Task Force on Litigation – all corroborate these defects. It therefore appears that the litigation system is not servicing the client needs although it remains the primary source of dispute resolution. The slow development of alternative A.D.R. schemes in Scotland (Citizens' Advice Bureau, Scotsman 14th October 1996) means that the court remains the main focus for resolution of civil disputes. In a competitive society the threat of a court action remains more powerful than a threat of mediation.

What Does the Court Provide?

A layperson would be forgiven for thinking that courts exist to provide judgements – decisions. Indeed that is implicit in Lord Mackay's list of standards. Lord Hoffman (1993:297) recognised that the bulk of court rules are designed to bring disputes to trial in an orderly manner. However many outwith the system may not realise each case has only a 3 to 5% chance of reaching the goal it is being prepared for – proof; 95% of cases settle at different stages on the pathway to adjudication. Three conclusions follow from this:

- in reality the court is not acting primarily as a decision-making body but as a focus for negotiation and settlement.
- the rule of law, pivotal to social and commercial worlds, is founded on a narrow distillation of cases, in many cases due to determined and tenacious litigants.
- trials before judges appear to be statistically insignificant in the final resolution of most disputes (Twining 1993:382).

It may be argued that these functions are acceptable and the court's public service is fulfilled, but it is the inconsistent and unpredictable patterns and reasons behind the 95% settlement rate which haunt a cost-conscious public service and create barriers to efficient management of caseloads, causing delays and costs for others (Lord Morton of Shuna 1995:2). This unpredictability also leads to overloaded court rolls with clients, witnesses and counsel waiting in the corridors for a judge, heightening pressure to settle at the latest stage, and creating a backlog of cases to be allocated a hearing. Again it may be argued that it is right that the service is demand-led, but increasingly there is a perception that courts have a wider responsibility than to the individuals who bring a case (Jacob 1986:264) and this 'new-age' attitude provides fresh challenges.

Challenges Today

There are three main challenges facing civil justice today:

- creating fair and equal access without increasing costs
- improving the quality, efficiency and effectiveness of court services
- controlling the costs, including Legal Aid, while ensuring adequate services

Taking the Scottish courts as an example, we can see that as in other jurisdictions, costs, delays and late settlements are inherent barriers to effective and efficient process. Finding the causal link is more contentious, although Lord Woolf in England has not been slow to blame the profession there for creating and supporting these barriers.

Costs

In Scotland no data on the cost of litigation are analysed and published by Scottish Courts Service. However 20% of cases initiated in the Court of Session and 46% in the Sheriff Courts are supported by legal aid, and these case costs have been analysed by the Scottish Legal Aid Board. The 1997 Annual Report shows that average case costs have risen 10% over the past year, and almost doubled since 1991, while the number of applications has fallen for the fourth consecutive year. The fee structure in the Court of Session has remained relatively unchanged for 5 years. Payments from the legal aid fund have actually doubled within the last 6 years while the number of applications has fallen 13%.

Years	Total Legal Aid Payments £m	Civil Payments £m	Civil Applications	Percentage Paid	Cases Supported
1991/2	79.8	16.6	33,200	61%	20,320
1992/3	109.3	24.1	36,000	77%	27,800
1993/4	124.4	27.8	32,500	85%	27,500
1994/5	132.1	30.2	30,600	84%	25,700
1995/6	133.4	32.2	30,300	74%	22,600
1996/7	143.1	35.0	28,733	77%	22,100

(Numbers rounded to 100s)

The Board attributes these disparities to a significant rise in case costs (1997:7), well in excess of the rate of inflation. The Scottish Home Affairs Department have stated that there is a need to refocus priorities within existing resources (quoted in The Scotsman 2 April, 5 July 1997), alluding to a suspicion that some members of the profession are deliberately spinning out cases and playing the fee structure. Section 53 of the Crime and Punishment (Scotland) Act 1997 gives the Legal Aid Board increased powers of investigation, but only for suspected abuses of *criminal* legal aid, tied to the increasing crime rate and an inalienable right to representation under Article 6 of European Convention of Human Rights. Wider measures of control by the Board and Scottish Office are anticipated.

In Scotland there has been no investigation of the costs for clients who are ineligible for civil legal aid (either through a means test or case validity); in 1995 they represented 80% and 54% of cases initiated in the Court of Session and Sheriff Courts respectively. No-one monitors these costs unless they are subject to taxation by the Auditor of the Court. Generally therefore the client is in an uninformed position of trust.

Delays

Delay is a relative concept (Zander, 1995:83), defined by the American Bar Association as 'any elapse of time beyond that necessary and reasonable to prepare and conclude a particular case' (1984: S.2.50–2.52). It is therefore an elusive concept. Delays may or may not be part of the bargaining strategy and tactical manoeuvring aimed at exhausting an opposing party, but are the outcome of four main factors which repeatedly defy rule changes:

- booking court and judicial time which is cancelled at a late stage, causing backlogs of cases waiting for timetable allocation.
- sisting an action which withdraws a case out of the sphere of the court – is this cultivated inaction or benign neglect?
- late and/or hasty preparation which results in repeated adjustments and amendments
- low priority in a busy caseload.

Where is the evidence of delay in Scotland? The Scottish Court Service publish annual Civil Judicial Statistics, rather belatedly. The latest issue shows the numbers of cases initiated and disposals during 1995:

	Court of Session	Sheriff Courts (Ordinary Cause)
Initiated cases	5,207 (6% down on 1994)	46,096 (4% up on 1994)
Disposals	3,899	35,189

These figures show case throughput only. No record is kept on time taken to progress cases. However, even from these basic data, the differences between initiations (by writ or summons) and disposals (those leaving the system by any route) illustrate that there seems to be a backlog building. This trend is reflected in previous statistical reports. We also know from the 1995 Report that 73% of the Sheriff Court cases leave the system undefended, requiring little court action, but there is no corresponding information for the Court of Session. Backlogs create queues which contribute to delay, but there is no research or published information in this area. There is no way of knowing how many and for how long litigants have been waiting for resolution. There is no information and therefore no impetus to push. There is no machinery to push. Some may argue that there is no right to push.

There are two further sources from which to glean information on time spent within the court system.

- In 1995 research was commissioned by the Scottish Office Central Research Unit on personal injury actions across 5 different Scottish court systems. Taking a sample of Court of Session Ordinary procedure and of the specialist fast track Optional procedure, the researchers showed that the average time to disposal was 72 weeks and 36 weeks respectively (p.37); 3 to 5% of cases were judicially determined in both procedures (p.30), the

majority of cases settling. The longest time cases were in process were 4 years and 2 years respectively.
- Lord Cullen's Review was supported by research on 300 defended cases disposed of during 1995, and previously unpublished data has been made available to the author. Corroborating previous research, 94.3% settled along the litigation highway, the remainder reaching final determination. The *average* time cases remained in the system was almost 2 years (94 weeks), but one of the most revealing comparisons is the dispersion – the *longest time* taken to a judicial determination was 4 years, while settlements stretched over a period of 9 years. Evidence of delay and a resulting backlog are beginning to be revealed. What lies behind these startling statistics?

Settlements

There are those who say if 95% of cases settle without interference obviously only 5% need management. They cannot be identified at the early stages, so why alter the system? (Zander, 1995:34). This viewpoint ignores the effect of realities of court practice on the client's decision to proceed. There are at least two problems which should not be glossed over. From the client's point of view, waiting years for resolution may eventually force settlement by stagnation, or emotional, physical and financial exhaustion (Genn 1987, Fiss 1984:1073). It may also stem from 'court-door syndrome' – a time when both parties' and representatives' minds are focused on the risk/benefit of progressing a case. From the court's point of view, particularly in the Court of Session, it is the stage of settlement which is vitally important. Lord Cullen stated that late settlements were the main cause of delay, wasted preparation, wasted administrative resources and caused unnecessary attendances (1995:3.3.8–3.41). How many settlements are 'late'?

- The Personal Injury study found that the most frequent occurrence of withdrawals through settlements in the Court of Session was just after time had been allocated for a proof (1995:5.12). In particular 41% of cases on the Ordinary roll settled at this late stage, 55% under the Optional procedure.
- In the Cullen Review sample of 300 cases, most settlements took place
  (a) after appointment to the procedure roll (13%) but before the hearing, and
  (b) between allocation and hearing of proof (51%).

Out of the 167 cases allocated a proof, the withdrawal pattern due to settlements was:

	Cases
Over one week before proof/jury trial	71
1 week before proof/jury trial	36
Morning of proof/jury trial	45
During proof/jury trial	4

In Scotland the Keeper of the Rolls allocates court time, and on a weekly basis has to balance a guesstimate of late settlements with judicial availability to minimise wastage. If a slot is not re-allocated, a judge could spend a morning in chambers. The Maxwell Report on the use of judicial time found that only 60% of judicial availability was taken up (1986:2.28), due primarily to late settlements (1986:6.46). Procedural reform is therefore aimed at eliminating the chaotic aftermath of late settlements.

Why does settlement occur so close to the hearing? In a recent survey undertaken by the author, court representatives were asked at what stage they emphasised negotiation and settlement to their clients. Of the total, 50% of solicitor-advocates, 75% of junior counsel and 80% of Queen's counsel placed emphasis 'before proof', in preference to the stage where the Record was closed. The general consensus was that the main deciding factor in settlement was the ability to make a realistic assessment of the strengths of a case after investigation and pleadings, based on a risk/cost analysis. Imminence of a court hearing was also a factor. The expectation of being called to court is part of the incentive to settle. There was also a general recognition that a realistic settlement could not be reached until all information was in, particularly from a defender, and this was 'almost never made available until shortly before proof'. Are these strategic meanderings or the results of late preparation since it is widely known that most cases will settle and not require presentation? Five factors emerge:

- settlements through stagnation exist (up to 9 years in Court of Session)
- settlement is on a risk-cost analysis
- information on which to base the analysis is not always available until a late stage
- imminence of a court hearing is a prompt for both client and representative
- late preparation and late settlements are symbiotic

Realities of Court Practice

Lord McCluskey said we must 'look at the defects which blemish and impair the true values which underlie our system' (1990:178), and this is a continuous process. Condoning a laissez-faire reactive system means that clients' needs are not addressed. Inefficiency means that the public purse is needlessly bled, and the practitioners' integrity is open to question. What Lord Cullen exposed was 'a culture of late preparation, unnecessary diversions, and a learned reliance on the indulgence of other representatives and the courts in allowing continuations and late lodgements' (1995:5.7). These are not newly discovered faults and have been exposed by previous investigations of court practice, both in Scotland and other adversarial systems.

Current Control

An investigation into Sheriff Court procedure in 1967 by the Grant Committee pointed to a 'lack of sense of urgency from sheriffs, court staff and solicitors' (1967:19) – this from a Committee which sat for 4 years. However they acknowledged that delays were caused by a lack of organisational control, particularly over the process of adjustment of pleadings. Progress was in the hands of the parties, and there was no machinery to police progress (1967:19–22).

In 1978 the Pearson Commission responded to criticisms of court procedure in personal injury actions and invited a Scottish Committee under Lord Kincraig to consider reforms 'to facilitate more expeditious and economic disposal of litigation' (Kincraig 1979:1). The average duration of a case at this time was 4 years in the Court of Session and 3 years in the Sheriff Courts. The Committee criticised the continuous adjustments and amendments to pleadings as a high contributory factor to delays (1979:6). The outcome was a fast track Optional procedure for personal injury cases, radically departing from the Scots principle of the dependence on full written pleadings which are prepared, adjusted and amended by practitioners. This innovative step led to an outcry over the loss of early debates on relevancy. But since the majority of debates fixed were not heard, the Committee had concluded that they were strategic and 'enquiry into issues can be postponed unduly by the need to dispose of preliminary pleas' (Kincraig: 1979.10). The most recent research shows that this track is twice as fast as the Ordinary procedure. The speed of resolution may reflect the success of abbreviated pleadings, but may also reflect the simplicity of the cases choosing to use this track. From another point of view, it has caused difficulties within the court system – 58% of actions are assigned a trial hearing, while only 3% are heard. This means that a higher percentage of cases are allocated proofs under this procedure and late settlements are more prevalent. These two factors combine to question the efficacy of abbreviated pleadings without further mechanisms to flush out the issues at an early stage.

Discharged Hearings

A 1995 Sheriff Court study (1995:4.22) corroborated the findings of the Kincraig Committee. Out of 269 debates fixed 27 were heard, 78% discharged on the day. Interviews with key court players disclosed that fixing a debate was

- a reflex reaction, particularly if there were no client instructions
- strategic, with no intention to appear
- a warning to the opponent that pleadings required amendment (1995:4.25)

Under the new Sheriff Court rules automatic bookings are curtailed, and the results of a post-implementation Sheriff Court study will evaluate the new rules in practice.

Lord Cullen also uncovered a pattern of discharged hearings – out of 82 cases appointed to the Procedure Roll in the Court of Session 70% were cancelled (Cullen 1995:3.11). He concluded (as Kincraig in 1979) that the diversions were 'an informal sist of process' (Cullen 1995:3.6). A sifting process prior to hearings had also failed. Practice Note No.3 1991, which required inter-party disclosure and discussion of arguments prior to appearance, had proved ineffective – 80% of appointments were cancelled (Cullen 1995:3.11). Practice Note No.2 1991, which required a pre-proof by order hearing to check readiness for trial and counteract the disruptive pattern of late settlements, was discontinued after 14 months (Morrison 1996:97). Since both practices were mooted as part of the judicial control of proceedings – why should there be a better chance of success now unless attitudes change?

Pleadings

The traditional practice in Scotland of combining the parties' cases in one key document – written pleadings – has been attacked as an instrument of prolongation, and is defended in its ideal form as a succinct precis allowing fair notice and flagging up relevancy issues prior to factual investigation. However, criticism of court delay has historically focused on the over-indulgence and reliance of parties on continuous adjustments and amendments of pleadings (Cullen 1995:3.29, Kincraig 1979:16). Again reality challenges theory. This leaves the legal profession, remunerated on hourly time basis, open to insinuations of incompetence and fee building (Morton 1995:2, Gill 1995:132) while purists argue that successful presentation relies firmly on perfection of the pleadings. This is the same pontificated role as witness statements which are accepted as evidence-in-chief in England and have swamped the English courts.

While Lord Cullen reported that the minimum time taken to complete adjustments and close the record of the pleadings was 15 weeks, the average time taken in practice was 38 weeks. The Personal Injury study in 1995 had found the average to be 43 weeks in the Court of Session, whereas the Kincraig Committee in 1979 found the average to be 24 weeks. Even if the time was perfectly justified, Lord Cullen's judicial dissatisfaction was compounded by 333 unopposed motions for late lodgments, pointing to a mutual indulgence between the parties and a culture of late preparation:

102 late defences
82 late open records
149 late closed records

This practice also extended to 190 motions to lodge amendments – 90 of them were lodged late. It is not the theory of written pleadings which is being attacked, but the practice (Cullen, 1995:4.4, 4.12). Settlements may even take place despite them:

> The vast majority of cases settle on a basis which has nothing to do with the comparatively minor issue which often absorbs both time and attention in the process of adjustment (Lord Rodger 1994:14).

Arguments over the need for time to respond and perfect the presentation of a case through pleadings are diluted by the potency of the criticisms of their eventual content. Lord Morton of Shuna criticised them as generally too long, extended by amendments, some deliberately obscure, verging on dishonesty (1995:2). Judicial frustration has been confirmed by the Inner House:

> Pleadings of the type currently used in the ordinary court procedure are frequently, and indeed normally ill suited to their true function, failing to put essentials in sharp focus, and often putting in sharp focus inessential matters of detail, which then become the subject of pointless procedural scrutiny. Lord Prosser ERDC

Construction Ltd. v HM Love & Co. 1996 SC 523 at 532 (sitting with Lord President Hope and Lord Kirkwood).

If this is the result of extended adjustments and amendments, the majority of them lodged late, how much longer is needed for perfection? Is perfection the goal?

Administration

Realistically the Keeper of the Rolls acts as a weekly resource manager in the Supreme Court, balancing judicial availability against the competing demands of High Court criminal workload, circuits, appeals, inquiries and civil work. From a base of 26 Supreme Court judges and an intermittent facility of 14 retired or temporary judges, a regular team of 5 to 7 judges are available for 40–45 civil trials and proofs each Tuesday. In 1986 the Maxwell Committee noted that the court timetable could be overloaded two and a half times available judicial time (1986:6.39). Since a consistent pattern of late settlements has become part of the working culture, the Keeper now allocates court time eight times the availability of a judge. Late settlements have become pivotal to the smooth running of processes (Lord Macfadyen 1997:58), although lack of judge and court may provide an additional psychological and financial pressure to settle on the morning of proof.

Calls for Management of the Litigation Process

Over the years piecemeal solutions and partial implementation (Lord Davidson 1992:130) have resulted in a gradual convergence of criticism of the adversarial ethos which underpins all common law jurisdictions (Resnik:1982:374), trapping professional and client in a system which has no overall management structure and suffering from conflicting agendas. Deviations from the ideal have prompted constant reform in a gradual movement towards increasing judicial control, balancing consumer needs with professional integrity. Overall trends are strikingly similar in Australia, England, America and Canada. It may seem that Scotland is following a fashionable trend, but judicial management is not a new concept in this country. We have not 'gone a-whoring after strange gods' (T. B. Smith 1959:4). Scotland has been moving in a staccato fashion towards case management principles over the past few decades, and has pre-empted the English Woolf reforms in its pilot study for commercial litigation.

Early judicial control, close supervision of disclosure and early preparation has been promoted as the ideal in every major Scottish inquiry into court procedure. The principles of case management are already in place in the Optional procedure, the new twin-tracking procedure in the Ordinary Cause Rules in the Sheriff Court and, more extensively, in the new procedure for Commercial actions in the Court of Session. The development of a vigorously interventionist approach by a single judge seems to be the inevitable culmination of piecemeal reform:

- The Grant Committee submitted that 'there should be timetables for the disposal of court business...fixed administratively and enforced with due regard to what is possible in a particular case' (1967:19).
- The Kincraig Committee concluded 'to avoid undue expense and unnecessary delays the court should have more control over the progress of the action' (1979:16).
- The Hughes Commission recommended 'giving the court a more active role in controlling conduct of the case than traditional in our branch of adversarial procedure' (1980:205).
- The Sheriff Court Rules Committee recommended that 'control and management of cases should be vested in the court' (1991:2, 4).
- Lord Coulsfield's Working Party on commercial causes recommended the nomination of a specialist judge to solve some of the 'familiar problems of the Court of Session procedure' (1993:10) in controlling the commercial caseload by 'balancing speed with a thorough examination of the issues' (1993:4).

It should be no surprise then that the Cullen Review found that 'the weakness of the existing procedural system demonstrates the absence of overall control and effective means of forestalling developments which can lead to undue delay and unnecessary expense' (1995: 6.15).

What are the alternatives?

There are several alternative/complementary solutions and sub-types, and each jurisdiction will settle on different combinations, measured against their fundamental principles and culture. These are:

- initiate a system of judicial case management, such as
  - differential caseflow management
  - administrative timetabling using time standards and goals
  - specific programmes targeting 'black spots' with new rules
- increase sanctions and professional incentives
- use information technology to track cases, alerting clerks to non-compliance
- encourage the use of alternatives – A.D.R.[3]
- originate all civil cases in the Sheriff Court under their new rules[4]
- redirect specific business out of court – large commercial disputes[5] or adjudication[6]
- do nothing – the civil caseload is decreasing, working practices are established

What is Judicial Case Management?

For Lord Cullen it is 'the adoption by the court of a systematic managerial approach to dealing with caseloads...differentiating between actions as to the procedural route which they should take' (1995 para 6.3), that is, differential case management.. The Ontario Law Reform Commission 1973 defined it as a comprehensive system of management of time and events as a case proceeds through the justice system, with two essential components – setting a timetable for predetermined events and supervising the progress through its timetable (1973:4). The purpose is to reduce delay, facilitate earlier resolutions in more cases, with concomitant reduction in costs. The theory is that increased access to the courts is facilitated by a broader range of the public, regardless of Legal Aid eligibility. There is enough in these ideals to give frustrated clients, consumer representatives and past Committees hope, but also enough to threaten those who are comfortable and unconvinced that theoretical advantages outweigh the status quo. With hindsight, it is naive to expect any transition to be welcomed. The system is imbued with, protected and shaped by centuries of legal principle (Black 1982:44), organised and structured around the adversarial ethos of party and practitioner autonomy.

Judicial intervention threatens the fundamental adversarial principles which maintain a judge's passive role. Early and continuous judicial control of cases is aimed at monitoring compliance with time limits and creating an expectation that events will occur when ordered. Traditionally the initiation and conduct of a case lies with the parties. Issues and evidence are selected at their instigation. Presentation and examination by counsel are specifically tailored to success. The momentum is controlled by the parties. Delays give time for conditions (e.g. medical) to stabilise, to raise money, reflect and negotiate. But party control has led to criticisms that the rules are used as tactical weapons to complicate and protract litigation in a contest of procedural skill (Sunderland 1926:729).

Roscoe Pound wrote that judges were hemmed in by procedural rules and handicapped by their roles as umpires in a search for truth and justice (1906:405). In Scotland we have hitherto embraced the principle that a judge acts as 'an umpire' awarding points as if a referee at a boxing match (*Thompson v Glasgow Corporation 1962 S.C.(H.L.36)*). In theory he or she intervenes only to clear up ambiguities. With judicial case management unfettered party control is subjugated to the wider public interest in an efficient and economic publicly funded service. Costs and delays are regarded as a hidden tax (Rodger 1994:9) and judicial management is seen as the key to efficiency. By changing the control system underlying the implementation of rules, and not just the rules themselves, Lord Cullen advocates changing the judicial uniform from referee to policeman. Fears are that this changes the entire system towards an inquisitorial foundation. Lord Cullen states that changes would represent 'significant qualifications' on the adversarial ethos (1995:5.3). Is this justified?

Recognising that other jurisdictions have voiced similar concerns, it is appropriate that we make ourselves aware of their experiences in implementing case management, while recognising our cultural and legal differences. Justice Ipp in Western Australia has written 'most of the problems are caused by the failure to adapt the adversarial process to modern conditions...changes to the legal system which do not affect that process will be cosmetic only, rather like attempting to repair a stalled motor vehicle by painting it a different colour' (1995:707). This comment may explain why previous piecemeal reforms have had little effect on efficiency in our own jurisdiction. We are paying lip service to changes, but not altering practices. We have been painting the car; Lord

Cullen proposed that we change the engine. To continue the theme – Lord Bingham M.R. stated that judges should be the engine of progress (1994:12) while in an adapted adversarial system the driving seat surely still belongs to counsel.

Is it worth the upheaval? A cool look at the advantages and concerns of those who have taken the soldier's leap[7] has revealed a catalogue of benefits and concerns, against which we can measure our own proposals for change.

Advantages of Judicial Case Management

A trawl of empirical, academic and judicial evaluations of the Australian and American experiences shows that although there can be no initial guarantee of successful implementation, the assumptions upon which Lord Cullen based his recommendations are grounded in practice. There is corroboration to be found, but piecemeal, and dependent upon firm commitment and co-operation. An amalgam of the advantages noted in practice in other jurisdictions are:

- early intervention crystallises issues so that areas of dispute can be narrowed at an earlier stage, reducing the number of amendments
- cases are fresher, better prepared, based on genuine issues and faults are picked up early
- within limits, cases receive tailored management according to their particular needs
- inefficient preparation is identified, reducing later disruption from inadequate pleadings
- supervision is maintained over litigants who chose delay rather than active preparation, weakening a structure of incentives to prolong
- there is greater trial certainty, less waiting time and less sporadic cost of preparation
- cases are called when considered ready, not on a first-come first-served basis
- appropriate cases for A.D.R. are redirected early on, clearing courts of small claims
- professional standards increase if the Court is scrutinising performances
- efficiency in lawyers' offices increases to match court timetables
- computer software issues reminders, reducing exposure to negligence actions
- costs and expenses are paid earlier, assisting practitioners' cashflow
- the less experienced practitioner benefits from guidelines through Practice Notes
- self-regulation rather than outside agencies control limited court resources
- accountability is increased – openness promotes public confidence
- a closer working relationship develops between judiciary, administrators and the legal profession
- major improvements in information collection have been noted, giving fuller and more accurate reports for informed assessments and policy decisions
- court performance standards and measures highlight areas subject to delays
- rapid and measurable inroads into backlogs are noted

Global Concerns

During the 1970s and 1980s pilot theories were tested in America concurrent with a fierce debate over 'managerial judging', particularly between Professor Resnik (1982, 1986) and Professor Elliott (1986). The open debate continues in confrontations between Lord Woolf and Professor Zander in England. However, Justice Ipp in Western Australia has noted that 'the intensity of the debate in America and Australia has subsided as results have underlined the salutary effect of the managerial judge' (Ipp, 1995:722). The New South Wales Supreme Court recently experienced vehement opposition from the legal profession during the development of a case management system but a follow-up implementation evaluation found considerable diminution of anxiety in practice, and positive benefits in lawyers' offices (C.J.R.C. Report 1995).

Professor Resnik initially argued that managerial responsibility gave judges greater power with fewer procedural safeguards. Lord Cullen acknowledged that an awareness of the pitfalls is critical to good management (1995:6.6). The Resnik/Elliot debate is re-enacted and expanded to illustrate the issues of principle which require to be addressed before implementation of case management rules.

Professor Resnik argued that substantive issues could be affected by procedural interference, although equally it may be considered that substantive issues can be affected by non-interference. By continuing the passive acceptance of unfettered access the Court is tolerating procedural tactics and inefficiencies. Non-interference may cause a backlog to build and settlement in many cases, not on substantive issues, but by financial or emotional exhaustion. Periodically the judiciary question the morality of their role. As Lord Bingham has asked 'is it right that there should be perfection for the few and nothing for the many?' (1994:5).

A forceful argument against judicial intervention is that consistency, predictability and certainty are casualties of individualised justice where judicial discretion is used to tailor rules to case needs (Atiyah 1978). The counter-argument is that under case management procedures decisions are based in the main on consensus after discussions between judge and counsel in open court. Decisions are open to appeal and it is important that judicial training creates awareness of potential dangers of personalised interpretation of the rules.

Professor Resnik also argued that the influence of statistics and time standards to measure judicial performance may lead to altered perspectives and goals. Judges' prestige may depend on efficient management, measured by speed and number of disposals. There is no doubt that information is critical to proper and efficient management, but it is crucial that both judges and counsel are also aware of the potential for seduction by court statistics and targets. Swift resolution may conflict with exhaustive inquiry into the merits of cases – a danger which has been recognised by all Committees recommending procedural changes.

Party control preserves judicial neutrality. Judicial control may lead to bias or perceived bias. The assumption is that although a judge is a passive observer in an adversarial system, he forms no views and makes no decisions until the case closes. Is this a realistic assumption? Under a case managed system there is a degree of judicial continuity and the question of bias is crucial, particularly if the judge is forceful. However, as practitioners in the Scottish commercial court have disclosed to the author through questionnaires, an early expression of judicial views can be helpful in evaluating settlement prospects.

Closely aligned to the question of bias, a major concern is that decisions can be made before all the facts are known. Judges may believe they know more about the merits than they do and intrude erratically, particularly if expedition is their goal. Here the counter-argument rests on the appeal procedure, resistance by counsel and judicial awareness of the pitfalls of early intervention. Directing procedure is a careful balance between promoting disclosure and efficiency and preserving a predictable level of party control.

Judges are trained and experienced advocates, indoctrinated into the traditional adversarial system – how many can make the transition to managerialism comfortably? Successful implementation is dependent upon judicial commitment and leadership, and consensus between judges of different ages and backgrounds is vital in a move away from learned principles. Also judicial prestige is in part dependent on their relationship with former colleagues and a managerial ethos challenges this relationship.

One of the major concerns to a court is an evaluation of the costs of a managed system – how do you measure a judge's productivity? There is no measurement standard. The same time can be used for disposing of 10 cases or a 3 day proof with a written judgement which sets a precedent for other cases to be decided in the shadow of the law. If disposal of caseloads are taken as a measure of judicial 'productivity' studies by Judge Flanders who headed 6 large American courts showed that twice as many cases were settled and tried using case management techniques than under previous procedures (1977:35).

Even if court process can be made more efficient and expeditious, a system which focuses on early preparation means that costs for the client are front loaded and truncated into a shorter period. Does this reduce access to courts at a time when Legal Aid eligibility is also decreasing? Early case management evaluations assumed that reducing delay also reduced costs. There is actually very little research which tests either this assumed correlation or the cost-effectiveness of different case management techniques. The reform process in England is currently addressing these concerns. An economic evaluation of differential case management in New South Wales Supreme Court (1995) has suggested that there is a correlative reduction relationship. The outcome of a larger study by the American Bar Association Task Force on Delay Reduction is underway, and together with the results of the English evaluation, will provide long-awaited evidence on cost-effectiveness.

Finally, early preparation and accountability may place additional burdens on solicitors and counsel with conflicting demands and deadlines. Smaller law firms may not be able to cope with work intensity although legal entrepreneurs may recognise the commercial value of offering clients a more predictable process.

Ultimately the decision to adopt a new regime rests on a balance of advantages and concerns, pragmatics and principles, the search for truth or adjudication – and costs. The equilibrium is a proportionate justice system which must embrace and evolve through the traditions and integrity of each culture.

Forms of Case Management

There are several distinct forms of case management and within these different packages are tailored to particular types of cases, complexities, claims and litigants. These include:

Caseflow management

This process involves a pre-trial conference, early judicial intervention to encourage early disclosure, narrowing the issues in dispute before allocating a proof. Generally one judge takes responsibility for the case from beginning to trial. The vital elements are court supervision from an early stage, setting targets for disclosure and amendments, allocating further interlocutory dates. This is the system used for Commercial litigation in the Court of Session.

Differential case management

To increase overall efficiency, cases are allocated at an early stage to different tracks according to their 'difficulty and complexity'. This system has been used in our Sheriff Courts from 1994. An evaluation commissioned by the Scottish Office has been due for publication for several months and will be compared with Lord Cullen's recommendations for case tracking using this system.

Time standards and goals

In 1984 the National Conference of State Trial Judges developed standards to measure timely disposition. The goal was 90% of civil cases should be concluded within 12 months of filing, 98% within 18 months, the remainder by 24 months. It is against these standards the American Bar Association's Task Force on Delay Reduction (adopted by ABA in 1992) evaluate the efficacy of different case management 'packages'. The aim is to balance time for individuals to develop their case within their procedural rights, while barring delay due to neglect by court or counsel.

Specific programmes

In Western Australia an Expedited List was set up to deal with a backlog of cases. Admission was through a discretionary judicial sift, procedure was based on early and intensive judicial intervention and standards and goals were set. Over 15 months 150 cases were admitted to the list, 80% disposed of within 4 months, the majority at the earliest stage. Early settlement was also achieved by New South Wales Supreme Court when 1200 cases were isolated for specific managerial treatment: 700 settled 2 weeks prior to the special listings, 500 one week before (Hon. Rogers 1993:98).

In 1990 America Congress passed the Civil Justice Reform Act 1990, implementing further delay and cost reduction packages throughout 94 Federal District Courts. Six case management principles and six guidelines were promulgated and the Rand Institute published a 5 year evaluation of 10,000 cases in January 1997. Reading Professor Zander's (1997:769) and Lord Woolf's interpretations (13th August 1997) of the results shows how polarised views over case management can be – also how selective cherrypicking from a three volume report can present both the case for and against judicial case management.

The main conclusions of the study are:
- some strategies reduced delay but not costs
- packaging the most efficient techniques may reduce time by 30%
- 95% litigation costs are uncontrollable by the court
- publication of judicial dockets reduce the number of older cases
- A.D.R. has no significant effect on cost and delay
- but combining early judicial management, reducing time for discovery, and setting a trial schedule early does decrease delay with a minimal increase in costs
- judicial time on cases increased marginally (on average by one minute!)

What both Woolf and Zander seem to ignore is that out of 3,000 judges interviewed in the Rand study, over 85% admitted that they did not change their management style and regarded the Act as a congressional infringement of their independence which was concerned more with the goals of speed and efficiency than justice. The results were therefore coloured, arguably negated, by unco-operative implementation.

Implementation in Scotland

A sweeping conclusion from studies around the common law world would seem to be that case management is like the curate's egg – good in parts. In Scotland there is a cumulative realisation that reform of some kind is inevitable, but there are hurdles to jump:
- The administration of the courts is by an executive agency which is an autonomous business unit run on the commercial ethos of the private sector, governed by financial objectives, performance targets and budgets. In 1995 there was an anticipated increase in workload over 3 years, but budgets were cut by £3 million. However there is a lack of co-ordinated empirical data to inform policy changes and implanting a business strategy on an unquantifiable service highlights the constraint between divergent principles of efficiency and justice. Justice becomes a proportionate commodity. Defining surrogate measures of performance and efficiency are controversial and require further elucidation (Peacock, 1994:22).
- Conflicting timetable pressures, heavy workloads and lack of real sanctions inform a working culture which weakens the link between formal rules and lawyer behaviour. As Lord Cullen noted, lawyers accommodate

84 THE REFORM OF CIVIL JUSTICE

each other (1995:3.6). The collusion lacks transparency. How much is attributable to the representative and how much by an unco-operative client? The Bar's submission to the Cullen Review exposed their fears over intrusions into their autonomous area, and their belief that the Scottish people would support their status. How much does the client need to know about court processing? The Australian Law Reform Commission recommend the practice of copying to clients all written requests for extensions and adjournments received from their lawyers to ensure that they are representing their wishes. The Rand Institute showed that inclusion of the litigant at hearings contributed to earlier settlements. It is rare for the client to be present in a Scottish civil litigation pre-proof and there is no direct information flowing from court to client.

- Lord Cullen pointed to the inadequacy of current sanctions for procedural policing (1995:6.34), and others have taken up his suggestion that the Bar and Solicitor-advocates should be found personally liable for abuses of process as in England (Cullen 1995:7.7). Current sanctions invariably fall on clients; few solicitors are found personally liable to the other side. The Scottish Bar, however, suffer no sword of Damocles. Glasser points out that a Bar which is isolated from commercial realities, with status and a secured monopoly, retards change while incentives for intransigence, entrenched attitudes and spoiling tactics may survive and restrict the pace of change (1993:318–324).

The theory that compliance results from dictatorial sanctions has not been borne out in England. Wasted costs orders, where the representing lawyer is held liable for unnecessary costs, have been unevenly applied and proved inadequate in their implementation (Scott 1995:23). They have proved an 'imperfect means of curbing excess by the legal profession' (*Freudiana Holdings Ltd. Re, CA* The Times December 4 1995) and led to numerous appeals. A wasted costs order is for improper, unreasonable or negligent behaviour but hitherto has not included pursuit of a hopeless case (*Ridehalgh v Horsefield [1994]* 3 WLR 462). However, under Rule 11 of the Federal Rules of Civil Procedure in America, the onus is on the legal representatives and their firms to give qualified guarantees of the quality of a claim (Schwarzer 1988:1014). Sir Richard Scott, Head of Civil Justice, is considering the possibility in England (Lawyer 1997:1). Lord Woolf proposes to develop Pre-Action Protocols governing inter-party communication before an action is initiated. Supported by costs and extension sanctions, compliance will be enshrined in Practice Directions (para 2.1–2.3 Civil Justice Proposals July 1997). Court powers will be extended into lawyers' offices.

What happens when parties are coerced along a procedural highway at the court's instigation? Appeals against the English County Court rules allowing the automatic striking out from court rolls after 15 months inaction (Order 17 Rule 11 CCR) have clogged up the appeal courts (see composite judgement for over 100 appeals entitled *Bannister v SGB plc* CCRTI 95/1410/G[8]). Justice Saville exposed the frustrations of the judiciary over a rule which was 'designed to strengthen the powers of the court, increase resources available, tailor orders to maintain effective control' but which has 'spawned satellite litigation' and increased delays totally opposite to its original purpose (1.2–1.4).

What can we learn from this 'lamentable history' (1.5)? We learn that compliance with rules of court may be influenced less by strict application of dictatorial sanctions than by consensus after widespread and appropriate critical consultation (Justice Saville, *Bannister v SGB* para 1.5).

There are inherent problems with enforcing compliance using rules to timetable case processing, and these have generally been recognised in Scotland without passing through the current English pain barriers. Kincraig pointed to an understandable reluctance of the court to insist on rigid compliance with timetables for fear of causing prejudice to clients (1979:16). Sheriffs recognised also that to become tough on adjustments might penalise the client rather than solicitor (Sheriff Court Study 1995:3.27). Without adjustments proofs are protracted (Personal Injury Study 1995:7.32), and both the Outer and Inner Houses have shown reluctance on several occasions to refuse late amendments 'in the interests of justice'. This is of course the key phrase which opens the door to late lodgements, and coupled with 'germaine to the case' is the ultimate weapon against judicial ire.

Sanctions are a necessary corollary of case management, creating an expectation that the rules must be complied with. Costs orders for the most blatant abuses cannot be ignored whichever system we adopt together with, it is submitted, fee incentives for front-loaded preparation. A heavy reliance on reform by coercion has not worked in other jurisdictions. Repeated adjustment and amendment practices and discharged hearings would not automatically fall within the 'improper, unreasonable or negligent behaviour'. Their Lordships have to decide where the boundaries of good management lie, although some argue that the declining standards of practice are actually attributable to the judges taking a more relaxed view of technical and textual criticisms. Given fresh sanctions, will the judges police the rules or will they demonstrate forgiving attitudes since they, above all, understand the work pressures of the bar?

This leads into another implementation problem – the judiciary themselves. Apart from the structural changes to their working week, advance preparation and competing demands of criminal and civil work, there are personal and psychological changes which will inform their attitudes to case management.

- they were all elevated to the bench from the Scottish Bar, trained and indoctrinated into the adversarial system – do they want to become interventionist?
- delays and costs have been part of the system for decades – is there a reluctance to interfere with the status quo?
- if they are interventionist in civil actions, can they revert to being passive in criminal cases?
- older judges are said to be dependent on researches of counsel (Hope 1992) – do they concur with the advance preparation required?
- decisions of the Executive, Legal Aid, fiscal policy, and resources to meet demands are currently outwith their control – how far can they influence these inter-related factors?
- judicial discretion is informed by individual philosophies and interpretations affecting consistency and predictability – can training overcome inconsistencies?

- continuity of appearance in a case is logistically difficult without increased resources
- no-one can accurately predict how lawyers will adjust to the new procedures
- there is no guarantee of success and they must all jump the soldier's leap together

Throughout the case management literature, the question is often asked – can a judge be a manager? The answer is inevitably another question – if there is to be some system of control, who else is trained to understand the substantive legal implications of procedural directions while balancing wider public issues – the profession, the administration, politicians, outside agencies? What will be new for the judges in Scotland will be lifting the veil of passivity and putting on the mantle of court governance – taking responsibility for the queues, the backlogs, the quality of the service which is promised both in the government's Court Charter and strategy statement of the Scottish Courts Service. It is difficult to imagine that all judicial expectations will converge and embrace the changes at a given time.

Can Case Management Work in Scotland?

The results of the current Scottish Office research into Sheriff Court rule changes will be coloured by different control problems within that system – primarily based on geographical disparities, the heavy criminal caseload and staffing by temporary sheriffs (Sheriff Court Study 1995:4.5). In the Court of Session in Edinburgh a pilot scheme for intensive case management has been running for three years under the commercial cause rules (Chapter 47 Rules of Court of Session 1994). Excused from criminal cases, the full-time judge controls his calendar and the pace of preparation at preliminary hearings, beginning within 14 days of the defences to encourage early disclosure, procedural hearings to prepare and narrow the issues for trial, debates over legal issues, through to proof.

The experiment has been an evolutionary process with constant monitoring of the impact of different techniques and ongoing research. An initial analysis was undertaken mid-term (Clancy, Murray, Wadia 1997:45). Continuous observation and more in-depth comparative empirical analysis by the author has shown why a single judicial docket system is the quickest and most efficient method for the court to dispose of cases, with little recourse to sanctions and few appeals. The disposals are within a much shorter span, at earlier stages, fewer cases are allocated to proof and the number of weeks waiting for proof is vastly reduced. However an increasing tendency towards late lodgement of materials in this court undermines early judicial preparation in a move towards reclaiming party control, testing the efficacy of the sanctions currently available.

Recent questionnaires completed by court representatives covering approximately 300 commercial cases reflect the nervous acceptance of the benefits of court control, but a rejection of intrusion into substantive issues.

The boundary between procedural and substantive direction is heavily reliant upon a judge's interpretation of an 'interventionist role', particularly where judicial discretion is supported by the Appeal Court (*Highland and Universal v Safeway*). A one-judge docket also has a limited life or risk personalising the law in a particular area. It is correct therefore that the full-time judge has been changed at the end of a three-year term. The heirs may flex their judicial muscles in a different manner from the ground-breaking pioneer whose agenda was to spearhead a radical new procedure against entrenched and sceptical views in a close-knit community (Lord Penrose 1996:1.06–1.07). Future research will highlight differences in continuity, predictability and consistency of interpretation and application of the rules. Is it the rules or the judge?

Comparing survey returns from practitioners, solicitor-advocates generally responded more positively to a procedure which facilitated early focus and flushing out issues in joint discussions, although junior counsel in this procedure tended to be involved at a similar stage. Queen's counsel were generally most resistant to judicial interference in 'the parties case'. Overall respondents were impressed with the speed, encouragement towards consensus, earlier disclosure and early judicial feedback. The drawbacks were, as expected, front-loaded costs and preparation, which altered the 'mindset' of the normal practitioner's presentation of the case. Pleadings had to be tighter, hearings were quicker, the strengths and weaknesses were tested at a very early stage and 'could not be buried under an avalanche of ordinary procedure'. This leads to 'prioritising preparation, as little work is essential on the ordinary roll until, at least, a procedure roll hearing'. This anecdotal comment is borne out by the settlement pattern of the Cullen Review sample – the majority clustered around the procedure roll and proof.

A more detailed analysis of the commercial procedure is in the stages of preparation, although the costs factor may be difficult to assess. For some commercial companies the benefits of a quick and final decision may outweigh early costs. However, truncating the preparation, work, expenses and judicial time may distort and hinder access to the general public, particularly those who are caught in the abyss between Legal Aid and a deep pocket. However, it may be argued that definitive early costs may actually be a more realistic assessment of litigation expenses, not hidden behind years of evasive and dilatory tactics supported by intermittent billing.

Lord Cullen has rejected the commercial cause route as too costly and labour-intensive for the resources available, while in England Lord Woolf has initiated a similar tight procedure for medical negligence cases as a half-way step to overall case management (Practice Direction 49 1996). It appears that individual judicial dockets are the vanguard of full-scale reform in both jurisdictions, which may or may not be confident predictors of the success of wider implementation. Apart from this experimental initiative, for the majority of actions Lord Woolf has chosen to create differentiated levels of judicial management proportionate to the amounts claimed (and cases on public policy issues). Learning from the commercial procedure in Scotland, it would seem more efficient from the Court's view to create mandatory specialist strategies for different types of cases rather than levels of claim, as the latter can be manipulated by parties to match levels of judicial control but the former may not. Empirical research may indicate specific areas for specialist treatment. For example, the 1994 KPMG study on court delay in England showed that approximately 40% of High Court and County Court cases originated from employers' liability claims and 40% from road accidents, although there are as yet no published statistics in Scotland.

However, whilst recognising the benefits of consistency and efficient disposal created by a one-judge docket, from the clients' point of view there are arguments against creating multi-tier access to litigation, dependent on the category of claim and resources of the parties. Discriminatory justice inevitably marginalises time and resources for those who lack the specific definition of their claim, arguably turning them into victims of court service. Specialist judges also deplete the judicial pool, testing administrative co-operation and support. Currently not all our judicial review cases can be allocated to the nominated judges and a new Patents Practice Note may be required to ensure that all patents cases now appear before the same judge. However, reorganisation according to type of action would justify Clerks of Court being allocated on a long-term basis to individual judges, building up the teamwork which supports and facilitates the smooth operation of the commercial procedure.

The Curate's Egg

Academic, institutional and judicial reports from case management jurisdictions appear to confirm that on balance the advantages outweigh the concerns. The advantages do not appear overnight. The concerns of the profession in particular must be addressed if their confidence and co-operation in rule changes is to be gained. At the moment there is an evident atmosphere of divisiveness between different court groups with competing agendas, and a lack of openness actually shrouds a morass of inefficiency. Lord Irvine of Lairg, the new Lord Chancellor, criticises this attitude – 'for too long in this country there has been secrecy for the sake of it, without principled consideration whether release of information will truly do damage' (4 July 1997). Unfortunately, as Sir Anthony Mason, recently retired Australian Chief Justice, said 'case management provides the service which clients think they are receiving already' (interview). The first steps towards preparation for any type of management must be lifting the veil, forming a common view of the service provided and working towards a consensual commitment to change.

By blindly accepting the settlement rates without further research and demonstrating a forgiving attitude towards repeated adjustments and amendments, the judiciary may be seen as condoning and colluding with the procedural abuses exposed by every judicial inquiry. Procedural tactics can hinder access to justice, and little more than anecdotal evidence is available to support reform policy. The lack of data leaves a weakness in the argument for case management.

The past three decades of continuous research and analysis of case management systems in the common law world has shown that there is no panacea – no single solution to reducing or preventing delay, cutting costs and creating access to justice (Church 1992:395). However, common features have consistently been identified in successful programmes. In particular, vital elements were identified in a cross-exchange of other jurisdictions' programmes[9] which independently had reduced delay and backlogs with the co-operation of the profession. These elements are:

- long term judicial commitment and leadership
- court consultation with the legal profession
- court supervision of case progress
- use of standards and goals
- monitoring and information systems
- listing for credible trial dates
- control of court adjournments

(Mahoney 1988:97–205, Solomon and Somerlot 1987:7–31)

Earlier American research which concluded that 'both speed and backlog are determined in large part by established expectations, practices and informal rules of behaviour of judges and lawyers – the local legal culture' (Church 1978:54), has been validated in practice. However the co-operation of clients, particularly sophisticated repeat court users, is not guaranteed. Their own agendas may overtake any efficiency drive which the Court instigates. Costs sanctions mean little at the expensive end of the market, and investments can be made above our judicial rate of 8% regardless of outcome. An opponent's financial status can be exploited, particularly if they are dependent on limited resources or even an overdraft facility, pushing them past the cost-benefit point of continuing a case. The pressure to settle is intensified at the door of the court where a party's apprehension and exhaustion may be further exploited. Settlements are also private, while courts deliver precedents which may not be in the interests of one or both parties.

Therefore while the court is placing the lawyer under an obligation to disclose information early the client may be instructing otherwise. This creates a conflict of duty between client and court which must also be addressed. Lord Rodger has stated that 'counsel has no duty to reform the law but only a duty to try to win his case, adopting a narrow or backward looking approach if that is the way to carry the argument' (1993:344). How does this sit with case management principles? The court has to ask itself who is the intended target of reforms? For whom does the bell toll (Rodger 1993:346)?

Conclusion

Although Lord Cullen's proposals fall directly in line with other jurisdictions' solutions to similar problems, it is submitted that drafting new rules remain premature. Underlying difficulties have to be exposed and addressed first, otherwise we may end up with a steady dribble of piecemeal rule changes, which, while being accepted in principle, are either unworkable in practice (as

90 THE REFORM OF CIVIL JUSTICE

with the pursuer's offer, withdrawn after 59 days) or absorbed and redefined by the established working practices of busy court personnel. The key to fundamental reform is balance – as Lord Cullen identified there is no need for full-scale intensive intervention, or dictatorial coercive sanctions. In acknowledging that attitudes guide the rules in practice, there are steps which can be taken to prepare the expectations of the players involved. These steps include:

- Policing the current rules before they are changed which will have positive benefits of
    creating an atmosphere of efficiency promoted by judges
    shaping the expectations that judges can fulfil their new role
- Undertaking an early analysis of sanctions and incentives
    testing case management principles within a guarded adversarial ethos
- Auditing process folders in the Court of Session (by an independent agency) to
    start judicial housekeeping
    collect and maintain accurate records
    track progress with precision by computer
    highlight consistent blackspots – for example incidence of sisting
    identify further areas for specific management
    identify older caseloads[10] for special sittings
    justify changes to profession, administration and Treasury
    corollary effect on public confidence
- Creating a case management portfolio of other jurisdictions' studies
- Initiating a multi-disciplinary Case Management Committee – there are too many conflicting independent variables attached to court reform (Edwards 1993:5,6). A one-dimensional analysis is not a healthy precursor of consensual change. While the Sheriff Court Rules Council has two lay representatives, the Court of Session Users Committee and Rules Committee are not representative of the community they serve.
- Re-considering the Hughes Commission 1980 recommendations, particularly for a Legal Services Advisory Committee, procedural judges and pre-trial reviews
- Considering creating a civil bench from those who are committed to case management principles
- Considering the expansion of specialist procedures for different types of actions
- Publishing guidelines which emphasise consistency, clarity and continuity
- Allowing clients direct access to information on case progress via a terminal operator

Taking a market approach and being client-oriented does not necessarily mean sacrificing the professional and adversarial status or legal principles – merely adapting them to commercial realities before they are no longer relevant to the public they serve. The new Commercial Cause Rules were specifically drafted in response to clients' criticisms and to discourage the use of private alternatives. Perhaps it is a measure of the success of this reform that numbers are rising on the Commercial roll, transfers from the Ordinary roll continue at a steady level and some companies are specifically nominating the Scottish court as the place of dispute resolution in their contracts. The underlying ideology is not new in Scotland. Lord Rodger has already noted that a predecessor Lord

President Inglis 'received adulation not because he preserved Scots law as he found it, but because he was innovative enough to adapt it to a new commercial society' (1993:344). And Sir Jack Jacob reinforces the point that 'the price of public confidence in the administration of the law is its continual renewal to match the needs of society' (1986:251). It seems therefore that legal procedures and principles will shortly be remoulded in response to critical evaluations of their effectiveness and efficiency. Reform is also defensive action. If the inefficiencies are not controlled internally, pressure from private alternatives or policy initiatives of a strong Government may sideline the Court's role.

> The government's aims of achieving a policy which ensures access to justice will be better served if we empower a wider range of bodies to protect the interests of those they represent (Lord Chancellor Irvine 23rd May 1997).

Since the Cullen Review was published two years ago, we have a new Lord President and a refurbished bench. Partial implementation has taken place, a business plan to support Cullen proposals is complete and a computerised support system is being installed. However, the main Cullen proposals have not been implemented. Current problems are still embedded in the daily operation of our civil courts while minor changes can be accommodated. It is only wholesale change to the power structures which have any chance of seriously challenging attitudes and working conventions which have defied previous procedural reforms. This means taking overall responsibility and control of potential areas of abuse while guarding fundamental principles. Who is qualified for this role – judges, lawyers, civil servants, or a combination? Reform which is dependent upon commitment and co-operation is also dependent on consensus. Consensus comes from openness, debate and logistical compromises. In every other common law jurisdiction case management has been a judge-led reform and some have entered into academic discourse to inform the debates. Lord Rodger has noted, however, that 'modern judges in Scotland have been less than conspicuous in academic debate' (Dublin 1994:13,14). Could this open the door to successful major reform?

If case management can work anywhere it can work in a small jurisdiction where most of the players know each other and are able to co-operate towards a common goal. In England, for example, there are 8,500 at the Bar, of whom 6,500 practice in London; in Scotland there are approximately 400, making cohesion logistically viable. If we tackle reform and get it right, we serve the client, benefit the profession in the longer term and become the flagship for the rest of the common law world. If we get it wrong, we can undermine the firm foundation we need for devolution. We may eventually have an autonomous Legal Affairs Unit in Scotland – will it follow the ideological out-reach programmes of the Lord Chancellor? Or will it remain insular, quiet and watchful while sitting on Pandora's box?

Notes
1. Prof. P. Sallmann, Managing the Business of the Australian High Court 2 JJA (1992).

2. Lord Normand, foreword to An Outline of Roman Law, T. Spencer Muirhead 1937.
3. See English Commercial Practice Note (No.2) [1996] 1 WLR 1024 increasing judicial power to remit to A.D.R. procedure or supervise early neutral evaluation of a case
4. Lord Rodger acknowledged the Supreme Court's role in creating clear and firm precedents (1994:12) which might preclude similar actions in the Sheriff Court.
5. Lord Prosser, Franco-British Lawyers' Society Colloquium 12 September 1997.
6. Lord Hardie, Franco-British Lawyers' Society Colloquium 13 September 1997.
7. A phenomenal leap to safety spurred by the adrenalin of battle at Killicrankie, immortalised in Scottish history.
8. Published for the first time by the Court of Appeal on the Internet, summarised The Times 2 May 1997.
9. Daytona Ohio Detroit Michigan Phoenix Arizona Fairfax Virginia Witchita Kansas.
10. If Lord Cullen's sample is representative, 12% of actions will be over 4 years old, equal to approximately 600 of annual intake. A special listing could clear most of these cases, or at least highlight repeated blackspots.

Bibliography

American Bar Association, (1984) and (1992). *Task Force on Delay Reduction Standards*.
Atiyah, P. S., (1978). *From Principles to Pragmatism*. Oxford: Oxford University Press.
Australian Law Reform Commission, (1996). *Working Document on Case Management*.
Bingham, Sir T., (1994). The Price of Justice. *Holdsworth Lecture*.
Black, J., (1996). Money Talks out of Court. *Scotsman* 14th October.
Black, R., (1982). Practice and Precept in Scots Law, *Juridical Review*; 31–60.
Cameron, G., Johnston, R., (1995). *Personal Injury Litigation in the Scottish Courts: A Descriptive Analysis*. Scottish Office Central Research Unit.
Church, T. A., Carlson, J.L., Tan, T., (1978). *Justice Delayed: The Pace of Litigation in Urban Trial Courts*.
Church, T., (1992). Old and New Conventional Wisdom of Court Delay 7 Justice System Journal **3**; 395–430.
Civil Justice Research Centre, (1995). *Implementation Evaluation of Differential Case Management inNew South Wales*.
Civil Judicial Statistics for Scotland, (1995).
Coulsfield, The Hon. Lord, (1993). Working Party Report on Commercial Cause Procedure.
Cullen, The Hon. Lord, (1995). Review of the Business of the Outer House Administration of the Court of Session (Cullen Review).
Davidson, The Hon. Lord, (1992). Law Reform – Who Cares? *Journal of the Law Society of Scotland*; 130–133.

Edwards, The Hon. D. A., (1993). The Role of Law in the Rule of Law, Presidential Address to The David Hume Institute November 1993 *Hume Occasional Paper*. **42**.
Elliot, E.D., (1986). Managerial Judging and the Evolution of Procedure. *University of Chicago Law Review*, **53**; 306–336.
Federal Rules of Civil Procedure, U.S.A.
Fiss, O., (1984). Against Settlement. *Yale Law Journal*, **93**; 1073–1090.
Flanders, The Hon. Justice, (1977). *Case Management and Court Management in U.S. District Courts*. Federal Judicial Center.
Genn, H., (1987). *Hard Bargaining*. Oxford : Clarendon.
Gill, The Hon. Lord, (1995). The Case for a Civil Justice Review: Contemporary Relic in Need of an Overhaul, *Journal of Law Society of Scotland*, **40**; 129–133.
Glasser, C., (1990). The Legal Profession in the 1990s: Images of Change *Legal Studies*, **10**; 1–11.
Glasser, C. (1993). Civil Procedure and Lawyers – Adversarial System and the Decline of the Orality Principle. *Modern Law Review*, **5**; 307–324.
Grant, The Hon. Lord, (1967). The Sheriff Court Report Cmnd. 3248 (Grant Report).
Hoffman, Sir Leonard, (1993). Changing Perspectives on Civil Litigation. *Modern Law Review*, **56**; 297–305.
Hope, The Rt. Hon. Lord President, (1992). From Maastricht to the Saltmarket, *S. S. C. Biennial Lecture*.
Hughes, (1980). Royal Commission on Legal Services in Scotland. Cmnd 7846 (Hughes Report).
Ipp, The Hon. Justice D.A.P., (1992). The Expedited List of Western Australia. *Journal of Judicial Administration*, **1**; 210–219.
Ipp, The Hon. Justice D.A.P., (1995). Reforms to the Adversarial Process in Civil Litigation. *Australian Law Journal*, **69**; 705–730.
Irvine, Lord Chancellor of Lairg,(1997). Keynote Address to Conference on Bill of Rights for U.K., London 4th July.
Jacob, Sir Jack, (1986). The Fabric of the English Civil Justice System. *Hamlyn Lecture*.
Kakalik, J. S., Dunworth T., Hill, L., McCaffrey, D., Oshiro, M., Pace, N., Vaiana, M. (1997). *Implementation of the Civil Justice Reform Act in Pilot and Comparison Districts*. Santa Monica, U.S.A. : Rand Distribution Services.
Kincraig, The Hon. Lord, (1979). Consultative Document on the Report on Procedure in the Court of Session in Personal Injury Litigation (Kincraig Report).
KPMG Peat Marwick, (1994). *Study on Causes of Delay in the High Court and County Court*, Lord Chancellor's Department.
Mackay, The Rt. Hon. of Clashfern, (1994). The Administration of Justice. *Hamlyn Lecture*.
Mahoney, B., (1988). *Changing Times: Caseflow Management and Delay Reduction in Urban Trial Courts*. Federal Judicial Center.
Maxwell, The Hon. Lord, (1986). Report of the Review Body on the Use of Judicial Time in Superior Courts (Maxwell Report).
McCluskey, The Hon. Lord, (1990). Errors and Omissions. *Journal of the Law Society of Scotland*; 178–182.
Morris, S., Headrick, D., (1995). *Pilgrim's Process: Defended Ordinary Actions in the Sheriffs Court*. Scottish Office, Central Research Unit.
Morrison, N., (1996). The Cullen Report. *Scots Law Times*; 93–100.
Morton, Hon. Lord of Shuna, (1995). Procedural Reform in the Court of Session. *Civil Practice Bulletin*, **1**; 2–3.
National Consumer Council, (1995). B.B.C. Law in Action Survey.
Ontario Law Reform Commission Report, (1973).

94 THE REFORM OF CIVIL JUSTICE

Ontario Attorney General, (1993). *Caseflow Management: An Assessment of the Ontario Pilot Project in the Ontario Court of Justice.*

Peacock, Sir A., (1994). Costs of Justice: An Economic Approach. *Hume Occasional Paper* **43**; 18–30.

Pearson, The Hon. Lord, (1978). Royal Commission on Civil Litigation and Compensation for Personal Injury Pearson Report. Cmnd.7054.

Pound, R., (1906). The Causes of Popular Dissatisfaction with the Administration of Justice *29 ABA Report*; 393–412.

Rehnquist, Chief Justice W. H., (1996). Year End Report on the Federal Judiciary, U.S.A.

Resnik, J., (1982). Managerial Judges. *Harvard Law Review* **96**; 374–448.

Resnik, J., (1986). Failing Faith – Adjudicatory Procedure in Decline. *University of Chicago Law Review* **53**; 404–460.

Rodger, The Hon. Lord of Earlsferry, (1993). The Bell of Law Reform. *Scots Law Times*; 339–346.

Rodger, The Hon. Lord of Earlsferry, (1994). A Civil Justice System in Motion. *Hume Occasional Paper* **43**; 9–17.

Rodger, The Hon. Lord of Earlsferry, (1994). Savigny in the Strand. *Inaugural John Maurice Kelly Memorial Lecture*, Dublin, November.

Rogers, The Hon. Justice, (1993). Supreme Court New South Wales: The Managerial or Interventionist Judge. *Journal of Judicial Administration* **3**; 301–320.

Sackville, The Hon. Justice, (1996). *Case management: The Australian Experience* (unpublished)

Schwartzer, M., (1996). Rule 11 Revisited. *Harvard Law Review*, **110**.

Scott, I. R., (1995). Caseflow Management in the Trial Court. *Reform of Civil Procedure: Essays on Access to Justice*; 1–30. Oxford : Clarendon Press.

Scottish Legal Aid Board Annual Reports, (1991 to 1997).

Smith, T. B., (1959). Strange Gods: The Crisis of Scots Law as a Civilian System. *Juridical Review*; 119–141.

Solomon, M., and Somerlot, D., (1987). *Caseflow Management in Trial Courts: Now and for the Future.*

Steelman, D.S., (1996). *The History of Delay Reduction and Delay Prevention Efforts in American Courts* (unpublished paper).

Sunderland, P., (1926). The English Struggle for Procedural Reform. *Harvard Law Review* **39**; 725–748.

Twining, W., (1993). Alternatives to What – Theories of Litigation, Procedure and Dispute Resolution in Anglo-American Jurisprudence – Some Neglected Classics. *Modern Law Review*, **56**; 380–392.

Wood, The Hon. Justice, (1995). Case Management in the Common Law Division of the Supreme Court of New South Wales 1991. *Journal of Judicial Administration*, **1**.

Wood, The Hon. Justice, (1995). The Changing Face of Case Management: The New South Wales Experience. *Journal of Judicial Administration*, **4**; 121–142.

Woolf, The Rt. Hon., (1997). Medical Lawyers and the Courts. *Samuel Gee Lecture to the Royal College of Physicians*, 13th August 1997.

Zander, M., (1995). Why Lord Woolf's Proposed Reforms of Civil Litigation Should be Rejected. *Reform of Civil Procedure: Essays on Access to Justice*. Oxford: Clarendon Press.

Zander, M., (1995). Are There Any Clothes for the Emperor to Wear? *New Law Journal*; 154–156.

Zander, M., (1997). Zander Replies: Woolf on Zander. *New Law Journal*; 768–770.

Zuber, Hon. Justice, (1987). Report of the Ontario Courts Inquiry (Zuber Inquiry).

Zuckerman, A. A. S.(1993). Reform of Civil Procedure, Rationing Procedure Rather Than Access to Justice. *Journal of Law and Society*, **22**; 155–188.
Zuckerman, A. A. S. (1995). Reform in the Shadow of Lawyers' Interests. *Reform of Civil Procedure: Essays on Access to Justice*; 61–78. Oxford : Clarendon Press.

Access to Justice : Lessons from the Sheriff Court?

D.R. Parratt

Introduction

In 1540, the Scottish Parliament of the time passed an Act ratifying the creation of the College of Justice, the forerunner to the present Court of Session. It provided, *inter alia* that the College 'remain perpetuallie, for the administratioun of justice' and devolved:

> to the President, Vice-president, and Senatoures power to make sic acts, statutes and ordinances, as they sall think expediente, for ordouring of proces, and haistie expedition of Justice (A.P.S. 1540, cap. 10.).

'Access to Justice' as a concept has been a powerful force in the regulation of civil disputes in Scotland since the sixteenth century. It incorporates the idea that civil justice 'should be available to all on the basis of equality, equity and fairness' (Jacob 1982: 277). Individuals are entitled to just and fair adjudication of their 'private' disputes by the courts. To this end courts must provide a defined and simple procedure which does not result in unnecessary delay and undue expense for the litigant.

It is argued in some quarters that the present system of civil procedure in Scotland does not meet these aims. Outmoded and 'a contemporary relic of a vanished age' (Gill 1995:129), there are criticisms of the fundamental bases upon which the system operates: the adversarial nature of the system results in unnecessary delay and resultant expense and nurtures a mentality which is not conducive to the resolution of disputes (Jacob 1988: 16, Gill 1997: 129); the emasculated role of the judge as passive arbiter or 'umpire' results in avoidable delays in the expeditious progress of litigation; the formal requirement of presentation of argument by written pleading adds to expense and as currently practised produces 'the antithesis of the candid, concise and lucid document' the system was designed to produce (Woolman 1997: 280). It is argued that for these and other reasons, the costs incurred by litigants and the public in general (as indirect funders of the system) have increased to such an unacceptable level that the system must not only be reformed but radically overhauled (Mays 1997, Gill 1995).

In recent years those responsible for the administration and smooth operation of the civil justice system have made a number of changes to the rules of civil procedure (e.g. Commercial Court procedure, Optional procedure). More are contemplated (Cullen 1995). Central to these changes (implemented and proposed) is the conceptual shift in the perception of the role of the judge. This article examines the changes which were made to sheriff court ordinary cause procedure in 1993 which incorporated a similar shift, the problems the changes addressed and attempts an assessesment as to whether they have achieved their objectives. Similar problems with civil procedure are perceived to exist in Court of Session Outer House ordinary procedure and Lord Cullen has recommended the adoption of changes, some of which are similar to those which have been implemented in sheriff court ordinary procedure (Cullen). Change may be required, but it must not be change for change's sake. The John Wheatley Centre has warned that wide-scale reform of our system of civil justice is not to be undertaken lightly (Wheatley 1997: 3). Before any radical reform is made, it may be prudent to take cognisance of the reception of the 1993 Rules changes which were implemented in the sheriff court.

Adversarialism and Defended Ordinary Cause Actions Pre-1993

Traditionally, 'ordinary' actions in the sheriff court were conducted in accordance with the principles of an adversarial system. In an adversarial system, the court plays a passive, non-interventionist role and the parties play a major, dominating, independent role, seeking to persuade the court to adjudicate in their favour (Jacob 1987: 7).

The adversarial system is often contrasted with the inquisitorial system. With an inquisitorial system of civil justice the roles of the court and parties are different. The court takes a more active, interventionist and authoritative role; the underlying principle being that the court is vested with the public duty and interest to ensure the proper conduct, content and progress of the proceedings. The parties' role is minor and supportive, assisting the court in ascertaining and determining the dispute (Jacob 1987: 7).

Prior to 1993 the sheriff's function included ensuring that court rules were observed and that progress of the proceedings was orderly and expeditious. His role did not encompass however, taking control of litigation once it had been brought into court (Macphail 1987: para 5–110). The pace and extent of litigation was largely the prerogative of the parties. As one Sheriff Principal remarked, '......the sheriff can exercise control but under the rules they are not explicitly required to do so. The sheriff can act legitimately as a neutral referee under the rules' (Morris and Headrick 1995: 27). This traditional role of the sheriff was viewed by many as hindering the expeditous progress of cases through the court which led to delay and expense. Another contributory factor was the procedure itself.

Three aspects of the procedure in particular were perceived as contributing to delay and unnecessary expense (Grant 1967; Hughes 1980; Morris and Headrick 1995: 13–15. C.f. Gill 1995: 129 and Cullen 1996 paras 3.6–3.20).

1. *Adjustment*: (c.f. Murray supra) Adjustment is the technical name given to the process of each party altering their case. After the

pursuer has stated his case in law and fact, and the defender has answered this, the parties are afforded a period for further alteration called adjustment. Adjustments by one party are often made in light of issues raised by the other side. Under the old procedure, adjustments were made by the parties on 'adjustment rolls' whereby cases called before the sheriff to allow him to see the extent of progress being made by each side and to grant further continuation where there were reasons for doing so. When both sides had completed their adjustment, the record (the document containing the parties respective final cases for adjudication) was 'closed', which prevented further adjustment and the case was sent for final determination. No time limit for the completion of adjustment was provided. In theory, after one continuation, further continuations of the case on the continued adjustment roll were only granted on 'cause shown' (which precluded continuation by reason only that the parties had agreed to it) (Macphail 1987: para 8–33). Although the adjustment and continued adjustment rolls were intended to provide parties with the opportunity to make alterations to their pleadings to focus and clearly define matters in dispute (Macphail 1987: para 8–27), in practice, the continued adjustment roll became a significant cause of undue delay. Parties often failed to focus the issues timeously, and on average cases were continued five or six times (Dailly 1993: 180). New issues were often raised at the last minute requiring further continuation to allow the 'intimatee' the opportunity to answer in the interests of fairness.

It has been suggested that the last minute adjustment 'syndrome' (c.f. Deutsch 1996: 8–9) prevalent at the time was due to poor preparation or as a result of tactical decisions both of which resulted in delaying final determination of the case. Joint motions for continuation were often granted without inquiry albeit that this did not conventionally amount to 'cause shown'.

2. *Procedure Roll*: This was the roll to which cases were sent for miscellaneous procedure e.g. for settlement and negotiation, minutes of amendment and answers thereto, the lodging of joint minutes etc. In effect it became a procedural lay-by. In the event that the sheriff refused further continuation for adjustment, some parties would attempt to continue 'adjusting' their cases by lodging minutes of amendment and answer on the procedure roll. Amendment is the procedure whereby parties seek to alter their case after the record is closed. (In some cases, fundamental changes to a parties' pleading prior to closing the record must also proceed by amendment.) A party wishing to amend must get the approval of the court before the amendments can be incorporated into the record. This would be sought ordinarily on the procedure roll.

3. *Fixing of Debates*: A debate is a hearing where the parties argue their preliminary pleas-in-law. Preliminary pleas are technical propositions of law which do not go into the merits of the case. If a party insisted on his preliminary plea, under the old procedure, the case was normally sent to debate. A significant number of cases would have diets of debate assigned but thereafter discharged at or immediately prior to the diet.

As a member of the Sheriff Court Rules Council explained:

> Another problem was that on average, eight out of ten debates fixed in ordinary actions did not proceed. This was another unnecessary step in procedure that was routinely used (Dailly 1993: 180).

Sheriff Principal Risk Q.C. has subsequently observed:

> As every experienced sheriff knows, the problem which existed under the old rules was the fixing of scores if not hundreds of debates which were never likely to proceed...........In many cases, when the record was closed, the fixing of a diet of debate meant no more than a three-month delay ......
> (*Dinardo Partnership v. Thomas Tait & Sons* 1995 S.C.L.R. (Sh. Ct) 941 @ 945D)

Morris and Headrick found that sometimes it was the delay *per se* which was sought and thus the debate was fixed with no considered intention of proceeding or as a second preferred option when further continuation on the continued adjustment roll was refused (Morris and Headrick 1995: para 4.25).

Reform of Sheriff Court Procedure and the 1993 Rules

The Sheriff Court Rules Council (hereafter 'the Rules Council') is a statutory body whose function includes keeping under review the procedure and practice followed in civil proceedings in the sheriff court (Sheriff Courts (Scotland) Act 1971 s.34(2)).

The Rules Council carried out a study of a sample of ordinary cause actions which had concluded in 1988 to investigate the extent of problems existing in sheriff court ordinary procedure. They also received representations from interested parties regarding undue delay, complexity and unnecessary attendance, and as a result the Rules Council decided to instigate a review of civil court procedures and primarily ordinary cause procedure. Their term of reference was: 'To examine the procedure and practices in the sheriff's ordinary court and make proposals for reform with a view to reducing delay, cost and complexity.' The Rules Council issued a consultation paper outlining proposals for change together with propositions upon which views were invited from interested parties (Consultation Paper 1990). Following consideration of the responses to the consultation paper, the Rules Council issued a report containing their conclusions (Report 1991) together with draft rules which became, with minor modification, Act of Sederunt (Sheriff Court Ordinary Cause Rules) 1993 S.I. 1993 No. 1956 (S.223) and which came into force on 1st January 1994. The rules implemented the Rules Council's five policy objectives for ordinary cause procedure. These were: 'cases should call in court only when necessary; the number of callings should be kept to a minimum; the rules should prescribe periods for completion of the various stages of procedure; the control and management of cases should be vested in the court rather than leaving the parties free to litigate at their own pace; and the procedures of the Court of Session and the Sheriff Court should be harmonised wherever possible' (McCulloch and Laing 1995: 24; Morris and Headrick 1995: 6–7; Mays 1997: 94).

The 1993 Rules attempted to radically alter the way ordinary causes were conducted in the sheriff court and in doing so the ethos which had existed under the previous procedure. As Sheriff Principal Risk Q.C. observed: 'The 1993 Rules have changed certain of the underlying assumptions upon which litigation is conducted, one of their main principles being that the sheriff should take an active part in ensuring the progress of the cause through the court' (Welsh v Thornhome Services and Ors 1994 S.C.L.R. 1021). A 'blow-by-blow' account of the rules is beyond the scope of this article, but for more detailed examinations, see for example: McCulloch and Laing (1995); White (1994); Mays (1997).

The rule changes were welcomed in many quarters and were viewed as innovative and 'demonstrating a line that could be followed with profit' (Morton 1995: 3). Lord Cullen in preparing his Review, visited sheriff courts to observe their operation, principally the innovative options hearing procedure (Cullen 1995: para 2.5), and noted that the rules incorporated 'elements of a case management system' (Cullen 1995:6.9). Lord Cullen subsequently incorporated the concept as one of the proposals in his Review. In the House of Lords, Lord Morton of Shuna, in a speech relating to the provision of civil justice in Scotland, noted that:

> There has recently been a radical review of procedure in the sheriff court, including a system under which the sheriff has much more control of the way the case proceeds and the speed at which it proceeds. Unfortunately, none of that applies in the Court of Session.... (Hansard No.1614: 183)

Some of the concepts introduced by the rules were not original:

In 1967, the Grant Committee, (1967, p.175) recommended that in order to avoid unnecessary appearances at court, 'there should not be repeated appearance for the adjustment of pleadings' and unnecessary attendance could be prevented by 'the institution of a timetable indicating with reference to the date of the service of the initial writ, the various procedural steps that the parties are required to take and the time for taking them.'

In 1980, the Hughes Commission (Hughes Commission 1980), considering the misuse of procedure as a source of delay concluded: 'It may be that a solution .... is to be found in the court taking a more active role in controlling the conduct of a case than has been traditional in our brand of adversary procedure.'

The 1993 Rules attempted to eliminate aspects of previous procedure which were misused and resulted in delay.

To counter the appointment of 'wasted' debates, a party wishing to debate a preliminary plea must prepare a 'note of basis of preliminary plea' and lodge it with the court not later than three days before the options hearing or any continuation of it (OCR 22). The sheriff will only appoint the cause to debate if, after consideration of the note in conjunction with submissions by the parties, he is *satisfied* that there is a preliminary matter of law which justifies the debate (OCR 9.12.(3)). It was envisaged that the sheriff would use this power to restrict cases seeking debate to those cases where there was *bona fide* reason for debate.

To counter the possibility of the adjustment period being misused, adjustment is time-limited after which no further adjustment is permitted (except with the leave of the sheriff). Rule 9.8 provides that the parties may adjust their pleadings until fourteen days before the options hearing or any continuation of it. The imposition of the time limit was intended to prevent the repeated continuations which had existed under the old procedure which had been the cause of unnecessary delay. The 1993 Rules do not provide for a 'Procedure Roll' or 'Miscellaneous Procedure Roll'.

The most significant change implemented by the rules, however, was the creation of the 'options hearing' which incorporated an element more commonly found in inquisitorial systems of civil procedure. At the options hearing the court exerts its control over a case by dictating future procedure including the mode of final disposal. The sheriff is under a *duty* to 'secure the expeditious progress of the cause by ascertaining from the parties the matters in dispute' (OCR 9.12(1)), as well as any other matters relating to further procedure.

The discharge of the sheriff's duty is reliant on the parties fulfilling corresponding duties imposed upon them. It is the duty of the pursuer to lodge a certified copy of the record with the court which contains the pleadings (i.e. the respective component final parts of each side's case) including authorised alterations, not later than two days before the options hearing or continued options hearing (OCR 9.11) and it is the duty of both the parties to provide the sheriff with sufficient information to enable him to conduct the hearing as provided for in the rule.

The sheriff reads the record prior to the options hearing and hears submissions from the parties at the hearing. Thereafter, the rules provide that the sheriff *shall* appoint the case to proof (or proof before answer if a Note has been lodged). Both of these are final hearings which deal with the merits of the case and lead to final disposal; or the sheriff sends the case to a debate if he is *satisfied* that there is a preliminary matter of law justifying debate. Alternative courses of action are available however. The sheriff *may* grant a continuation of the options hearing for a period not exceeding 28 days (or first suitable court day thereafter). There can be only one continuation of the options hearing. This is designed to prevent the recurrence of numerous continuations prevalent under the previous procedure. The sheriff *may* order the case to proceed under Additional Procedure if he is *satisfied* as to its difficulty or complexity. As its name suggests, this is a procedure which allows the parties further procedure to clarify the issues in dispute and is designed to deal with cases of such complexity that they cannot reasonably be completed within the ordinary time frame. Finally, if a party is in default, the sheriff *may* grant decree as craved, decree of absolvitor or dismiss the cause with expenses, as the case may be. The ambit of situations in which a party is held to be in default is defined in Rules 16.2 (ordinary procedure) and 33.37 (family procedure). It includes the failure to lodge, or failure to intimate the lodging of any production or part of process within any time period provided for by the rules or by the sheriff. Also, failure to implement an order of the sheriff or failure to appear or to be represented at any diet (i.e. court date) will result in default. Therefore, if one or either of the parties fail to 'obey' the rules they will be deemed to be in default. For example, if the pursuer does not lodge the record timeously prior to the options hearing, the pursuer is in default. When a party is in default the sheriff may grant decree against him. Of the decrees the sheriff can grant, the first two decrees are final decrees. Respectively, neither the defender nor the pursuer can come back to court. They have lost the action. This is a very severe sanction. All they may do is appeal to a higher court. If the case is dismissed, the aggrieved party may come back to the court and re-start the action from the beginning. He has to re-incur previous expense to bring the action back to its point of dismissal. If the sheriff dismisses the cause with expenses, the party must pay, in whole or part, the expenses run up by his opponent from the start to the point of dismissal as well as his own.

Late Records, Dispensing Power and the Expeditious Progress of the Cause

A party who fails to comply with the rules and is held to be in default can appeal to the sheriff to be excused. He must have a *bona fide* reason or reasons for his failure. He must explain to the sheriff the reason(s) and then move the sheriff to grant relief from the consequences of his default by exercising the dispensing power under Rule 2.1. Whether relief is granted thereafter is a matter for the sheriff's discretion.

At the time the rules were introduced, it was envisaged that in most cases a proof would be assigned following the options hearing (SCRC Report 1991; Civil Judicial Statistics 1995) and in general, no continuation of the options hearing would be permitted (Neilson 1993). Some sheriffs were provided with ideas by members of the Sheriff Court Rules Council prior to implementation of the rules as to the pro-active approach they were to take (Johnston 1995a: 5).

As the rules were implemented, it became apparent, perhaps not surprisingly, that parties, (or more correctly their advisors) were failing to meet the time limits imposed by the rules. A particular problem was the failure by parties to comply with OCR 9.11 (the lodging of the record before the options hearing) which hindered the sheriff discharging his pro-active duty. Although in theory, every case turns on its own merits, the courts, principally the appellate courts of the Sheriffs Principal, sought to establish parameters and to give guidance and clarification as to the practical approach to be adopted. This originally lead to a bifurcated approach as to the sanctions which fell to be imposed for default. The following interpretation came to be known as the 'strict or hard approach.'

The 'Strict' or 'Hard' Approach

The courts noted that the Ordinary Cause Rules 1993 provide that the sheriff's function at the options hearing is to 'seek to secure the expeditious progress of the cause' and it was therefore essential that the options hearing operated efficiently to secure this objective (*D.T.Z. Debenham Thorpe v Henderson Transport* 1995 S.L.T. 553; 1995 S.C.L.R. 345). The sheriff's role is a pro-active one, and to discharge this, the sheriff must firstly prepare for the options hearing by reading the record prior to the hearing. Therefore, it is 'crucial' or 'vital' that the record is lodged with the court to permit the sheriff the necessary time to prepare (Welsh; *Group 4 Total Security Ltd v Jaymarket Developments Ltd* 1996 S.L.T. (Sh Ct) 61; 1995 S.C.L.R. 303; D.T.Z. Debenham Thorpe; *Morran v Glasgow Council of Tenants' Associations* 1995 S.L.T. (Sh Ct) 46; 1994 S.C.L.R. 1065). Default in not lodging the record timeously affects not only the parties, but also the court and cannot be disposed of by granting more time or by making a finding of expenses (D.T.Z. Debenham Thorpe), nor can the sheriff merely continue the options hearing to accommodate the late record as firstly he has no information before him to permit such a course and secondly, this would be a corruption of the procedure (Group 4). Continuations will only be granted if parties provide a persuasive reason for requiring further continuation, which does not include a submission that the parties are agreed as to further continuation (*Mahoney v Officer* 1995 S.L.T. (Sh Ct) 49; 1994 S.C.L.R. 1059; Welsh).

If the record has not been lodged then the party is in default and the sheriff may grant decree of dismissal by default at the options hearing. Granting decree of dismissal however does not cause substantial injustice as a party may return to court and re-raise the action (Mahoney). Decree of Absolvitor is normally a sanction wholly disproportionate to the default (Group 4).

However, the sheriff always has a discretion as to whether he grants decree (D.T.Z. Debenham Thorpe). The sheriff may excuse the default by exercising the 'dispensing power' in provided in Rule 2.1. If his decision is appealed, the question for an appellate court in reviewing the exercise of that discretion is whether the sheriff has misdirected himself in law, or has failed to take into account a material and relevant factor or has reached a wholly unreasonable result (D.T.Z. Debenham Thorpe).

The 1993 Rules differ from the previous ordinary cause rules in that a party must show that a failure to comply with the rules was due to 'mistake, oversight or other excusable cause.' Whether the explanation given is 'excusable' must be interpreted within the framework and philosophy of the 1993 rules (Morran). An unfamiliarity with the rules does not amount to a satisfactory excuse for a failure to lodge a record (*De Melo v Bazazi* 1995 S.L.T. (Sh Ct) 57; 1995 S.C.L.R. 564), but may be sufficient to excuse failures to meet other time limits.

In considering whether to relieve the party from the consequences of default, the sheriff must also consider the consequences of dismissal. If it is not in the interests of justice to dismiss the action (e.g. because the action becomes time-barred) or the action is not a simple or is an unusual one (*D. A. Baird v*

Nisbet & Anr 1995 S.C.L.R. 1127) the sheriff may grant relief. A balance must be struck between the gravity of the default and the consequences of granting decree of dismissal (*Price v Fernando* 1995 S.C.L.R. 23).

A strict approach to the interpretation of the 1993 Rules is necessary as excuses can easily be found for failure to comply and if they are accepted in one case, in equity they must be accepted in other cases. Hard decisions are sometimes necessary if the rules are to operate properly. Failure to lodge a record is not a trivial matter, nor is it lightly excused, nor excused as a matter of course (Group 4).

This 'strict or hard approach' embraced a Procrustean attitude adopted by the appellate courts in their interpretation of the provisions of the 1993 Rules and may have been informed by a fear that the new rules would be interpreted in practice in such a way as to incorporate many of the bad practices which had existed under the previous rules. The rules were formulated, as has been seen, to prevent the use (or misuse) of procedure to hinder the expedition of cases through the court. The over-riding concern has been the retention of control of the pace of litigation by the court. As Mays (1997) has noted, the dismissal of actions for procedural defaults appears *prima facie* incongruous with the declared intention of the rules to expeditiously progress cases and to eliminate delay and it is questionable whether overall expedition and substantive justice is served by the enforcement and rigorous application of the procedure. Further, the dismissal of cases normally results in the penalisation of the parties themselves as opposed to their legal advisors. Such considerations informed an alternative interpretation of the 1993 Rules relating to the default of failing to lodge a record for an options hearing.

The 'Soft' or 'Lenient' approach

In the initial flurry of decisions following implementation, a 'softer' or more 'lenient' approach was expounded by the Sheriff Principal of South Strathclyde, Dumfries and Galloway (*Burtonport Fishermen's Co-operative v Sans Unkles* 1994 S.C.L.R. 844; *Strathclyde Business Park (Management) Ltd v Cochrane* 1995 S.L.T. (Sh Ct) 69) incorporating a 'bird's eye view' of the expeditious progress of a cause. The Sheriff Principal considered that the unjustified dismissal of cases did not expedite them and incurred expense as well as delay in the resolution of a dispute by bringing the pursuer back to the start (Strathclyde Business Park). He considered that a dismissal would have to be justified in accordance with conventional principles. In Burtonport, the Sheriff Principal held that dismissal of the action for a failure to lodge a record was unreasonable as again the pursuer would have to start again resulting in further delay in the resolution of the dispute which was not the object of the 'new' rules. He considered that the court should have adjourned the hearing for the record to be lodged.

This soft or lenient approach was subsequently criticised by other sheriffs principal on three grounds: firstly, it is founded conceptually in the position which existed before the 1993 Rules and does not take account of the change of emphasis in the 1993 Rules (D.A. Baird); secondly, an adjournment would be a continuation within the meaning of OCR 9.12 and would preclude further continuation for a 'legitimate purpose' (Group 4); and thirdly, it fails to impose an effective sanction for failure to obtemper OCR 9.11 (Group 4). However, as seen below, although this approach has been discredited theoretically, there are suggestions it is more readily adopted at a practical level.

The 1993 Rules in Practice and Associated Problems

Practitioner Attitudes and the Culture of Reception

Reflecting on Lord Woolf's proposed changes to English civil procedure, Scott has observed:

> The impact that they will have on the way civil cases develop cannot accurately be predicted. Further, the ways in which parties, and more particularly litigation lawyers will adjust to this remains to be seen. Their resourcefulness and their capacity for good reasons and bad, to undermine the best laid plans should not be underestimated (I.R. Scott in Zuckermann & Cranston (1995): 29).

Remarking on the 1993 Rules, the pro-active role imposed on the sheriff, and attitudes to the rules Mays has said:

> It is debatable to what extent the options hearing has truly transformed civil litigation in sheriff court ordinary actions. Anecdotal evidence would suggest that the options hearing has not revolutionised practitioner attitudes to the process of litigation but rather that many old attitudes and approaches are now accommodated within the confines of the new procedure (Mays 1997: 97).

The absence of published research makes it difficult to assess to what extent the 1993 Rules have achieved in practice the objectives which underpinned their creation. Their success was always likely to be dependent on the attitudes of the bench and profession. Observations by sheriffs principal, sheriffs and solicitors in the literature and reported cases, however, would seem to suggest that the Rules have not been as successful as the Rules Council might have envisaged. This might partly be explained by the fact that radical reforms usually produce unexpected, unwelcome results (Zander 1995), but it is of greater importance that the changes to the Ordinary Cause Rules were not initially universally welcomed by the profession. As Mays has commented: 'at the time of implementation, and for a period thereafter, the new ordinary cause procedure proved substantially unpopular' (Mays 1997: 96). The reasons for this unpopularity are probably varied. It may have resulted from the novel proposition that it was no longer possible for parties to dictate the pace of litigation. Another plausible explanation for the 1993 Rules being unpopular may be that a perception existed that there had been little wrong with the old procedure. The Edinburgh Bar Association, after the 1993 Rules had been in force for one year, canvassed the views of its civil litigation members as to the changes and noted:

While many representatives appeared to take a relatively neutral view as to whether the new rules represented a change for the better, significantly not one single respondent expressed a view that the system was operating more smoothly than was previously the case and several senior practitioners wholeheartedly condemned the rules as being a backward and retrograde step. (Recommendations of Edinburgh Bar Association 1995: 1).

The imposition of time limits for the completion of parts of procedure also caused concern (c.f. views expressed by practitioners prior to implementation. Headrick and Morris 1995: 13–14). The view amongst some practitioners was that the rules had become a 'procedural minefield' (Mays 1997: 97); making the lives of sole practitioners a misery (Vocational Training Unit Seminar: Discussion) and in general, failing to take account of the practicalities of the day-to-day running of solicitors' offices operating within a commercial environment. The requirement to lodge a record two days before the options hearing under pain of possible dismissal was criticised in particular on the basis that it put solicitors and their staff under 'intolerable strain' (Recommendations of Edinburgh Bar Association 1995: 3).

It had been thought that the 1993 Rules would encourage parties in the early preparation of their case. Last minute preparation had been not unusual under the previous procedure. As the Hughes Commission noted 'There is a human tendency for even the most responsible professionals, if they are busy men, to put off work which can wait' (Hughes Commission 1980: 205). 'The natural human tendency to leave everything to the last minute' (Deutsch 1996: 10), however, has probably continued to have an effect on the 1993 Rules in practice and it is open to question whether the aim of early preparation has been achieved.

Shrieval Interpretation, Substantive Justice and Procedural Compliance

Any approach taken by a sheriff will be according to his vision of the ethos and underlying principles of the 1993 Rules. The rules enjoin the sheriff to 'secure the expeditious progress of the cause' (OCR 9.12). Further, he has fairly broad powers under Chapter 2 to relieve parties from the consequences of failures and defaults. In both these respects the sheriff will act according to his personal perception of how the rule should be applied. Necessarily his approach will be tempered by any approach taken by his sheriff principal as well as by similar decisions of the Court of Session which he is bound to follow. He may acknowledge the persuasiveness of approaches adopted by other sheriffs principal (which are not binding on him). In practice, however, the sheriff will have a wide latitude, perceived or otherwise, to act according to the principles underlying the rules as he thinks best in all the circumstances. As Sheriff Kelbie has noted, as the operation of (options hearings) depends on the approach of the sheriff, 'it is not surprising that there appear to be differences, even among sheriffs principal, in the decisions' (Kelbie 1995: 7). Implicit in the introduction of the 1993 Rules was the idea that a new approach would harmonise the conduct of litigation in the sheriff court throughout Scotland (Dailly 1993:

180), and that the 'pro-activity' imposed on the sheriff, whilst allowing a beneficial degree of flexibility, would be used to ensure the efficient and expeditious progress of cases through the ordinary court. In practice, there would appear to be some variations of practice among sheriffs principal, sheriff courts and sheriffs.

Predictably perhaps, this has reached it's zenith (or nadir) at the point in the procedure where the sheriff has greatest discretion, i.e., at the options hearing. Whilst 'idiosyncrasies are part and parcel of the sheriff court' (Johnston 1995: 5), if the approaches of sheriffs lack consistency, collectively they will also lack predictability and a justifiable complaint among practitioners has been that it is now important to 'know your sheriff' (Johnston 1995: 5). Sheriffs take differing approaches at options hearings in the situation where the pursuer has failed to lodge the record timeously and this has frustrated the objects of the rule. The 'strict approach' would require the sheriff to dismiss the case unless the party moves him to exercise the dispensing power, and the sheriff, in all the circumstances, considers it justifiable to do so. A study conducted by the writer (illustrative rather than representative), found that whilst the incidence of failures to lodge records following the implementation of the 1993 Rules has remained relatively consistent, the incidence of dismissal has remained relatively low, sheriffs preferring if possible to accommodate the late record and impose a sanction other than dismissal. This was of course part of the (discredited) 'soft' approach.

Administrative Discrepancies

Discrepancies have arisen administratively as to whether the record can be received after the period for lodging has elapsed. The Rules provide that the record must be lodged two days before the options hearing and a shrieval decision (*Ritchie v Maersk* 1994 S.C.L.R. 1038) confirmed that this meant two 'clear' days after which the party is deemed to be in default. It is understood that some sheriff courts have therefore refused to accept the record if the time limit has expired. Other sheriff courts however have taken a more lenient approach and have received the record, placing it with the papers for the sheriff but marking it as 'tendered' as opposed to 'lodged' (i.e. marking that there has been a failure to obey the rule as to timeous lodging but the record is still placed with the rest of the papers). The sheriff is therefore alerted to the fact that there has been a default in terms of the rules as the record is marked by the sheriff clerk as 'tendered'. This approach permits him the opportunity of preparing for the options hearing by reading the late record and thereafter addressing the default at the options hearing.

It is understood that some sheriff courts have considered that the record can competently be lodged *on* the second day prior to the options hearing. The issue was muddied when it arose before the Inner House in D.T.Z. Debenham Thorpe. The approach in Maersk was followed but the Inner House considered that a degree of latitude is permissible when the rule operates in practice.

Aberration and Innovation

It has been argued that there has also been reluctance on the part of sheriffs to act according to the principles of the strict approach which has led at best to straining the interpretation of the provisions of the 1993 Rules and at worst innovation in their application. Although Sheriff Principal Risk considered that the continuation of the options hearing for the accommodation of a late record was a clear aberration of procedure (Group 4), in seeking to act expeditiously, anecdotal evidence would suggest that some sheriffs have on occasion adopted such a course. Further, at the continued options hearing, in some cases the hearing has been continued again to a 'third options hearing' (e.g. Letter to the Editor, Greens Civil Practice Bulletin Issue 10: 11) or the court has engaged in the fiction of 'discharging and re-assigning' the options hearing (e.g. Johnston 1996c: 5). The writer's research suggests that this is not a common practice. However, the inherent danger in such courses being adopted is that they implicitly condone aberrations of procedure. Such considerations were responsible for the frequent continuations of cases under pre-1993 procedure (e.g. continuations not on 'cause shown' but on joint motion). It may be that in some circumstances, the interests of justice require aberration or innovation but these instances should be exceptional. Difficulties will always arise for a sheriff in marrying substantive justice and procedural compliance.

The Return of the Procedure Roll

An unfortunate addition to the 1993 Rules in some sheriff courts has been a re-creation of the 'old' Procedure Roll. This was the Roll under the old procedure which had been a contributory factor to delay endemic at the time. As has been noted, the 1993 Rules do not provide for one. Commenting on an interlocutor which continued a cause to the 'Additional Procedure Roll', Sheriff Principal Maguire Q.C. said:

> This is not a creature with which I am familiar........While I accept that not all cases can proceed as smoothly as is envisaged in the Ordinary Cause Rules 1993 and there is on occasion necessary continuation to hearings to consider Minutes of Amendments and the like, I would discourage the setting up of Additional Procedure Rolls or Miscellaneous Procedure Rolls. If the Court provides a haven, cases will inevitably seek shelter there. This will generally be of benefit to the incompetent, inefficient or the merely idle. The courts would then gradually revert to the pre 1993 attitudes. This should not be allowed to happen. It is for Sheriffs to take charge of the cases so far as they can, and ensure that the case proceeds as expeditiously as possible. (*Smart v. Tullis Russell Ltd* unreported 18th June 1996).

A very different view, however, was promulgated by the Edinburgh Bar Association:

> it has been noted that Glasgow Sheriff Court has instituted a Miscellaneous Procedure Roll which appears to be quite inconsistent with anything in the new rules, and it is understood that Dundee Sheriff Court now has a Procedure Roll.

That may be inconsistent with the content of the new rules but it is utterly consistent with logic and pragmatism. (Edinburgh Bar Association 1995:10).

The writer is not aware of the number of 'procedure rolls' which have been re-created in all the sheriff courts. It would follow, however, that if they are in existence, there is some force in Sheriff Principal Maguire's argument, especially if the adjustment period is not utilised effectively.

Adjustment and Amendment and Delay Displacement

The 1993 Rules provide that for a minimum of six weeks adjustment takes place between the parties and must conclude fourteen days before the options hearing. Further adjustment is permitted between the options hearing and any continuation of it but again must be completed fourteen days before the continued options hearing (in essence permitting a continued period of adjustment of two weeks).

It would appear that in some courts, parties are increasingly intimating adjustments on, or near the last day permitted for adjustment (Deutsch 1996: 8; Johnston 1996: 6–7). This might be due to genuine last minute developments requiring last minute incorporation or as a result of last minute preparation or tactical decisions taken by one party seeking further continuation (Deutsch 1996: 8–9). Whatever the motive, if the adjustments made by one party are significant and are made on the last day permitted prior to a continued options hearing, the sheriff is faced with the difficulty of either refusing a party the opportunity of answering matters raised by an opponent (by legitimate means) and progressing the action to its next natural step or seeking to accommodate within the time frame the opportunity to answer the adjustments by amendment after the record is closed at the continued options hearing and fixing a diet of final procedure. The first approach is difficult to reconcile with the interests of justice and with the second approach, the decision as to final procedure may ultimately be frustrated by the dynamics of parties altering their respective cases. After minutes of amendment and answer, parties are sometimes permitted further 'adjustment' in light of them. OCR 18.3 provides that where the sheriff allows adjustment to the minutes he shall fix a date for hearing the parties on the minutes and adjustments. Both must be lodged with the court prior to the hearing (*Bryson v Gresham* 1996 S.C.L.R. 776). It is open to question whether the sheriff has the same pro-active powers at such a hearing The sheriff held that he retained similar powers in the decision of Bryson on the basis that the whole procedure under the 1993 Rules could be called into question by parties lodging minutes of amendment.

An analogy with the practice under the previous procedure is apposite. With the pre-1993 rules, delay was caused by lengthy adjustment and by the fixing of debates which were then discharged and re-assigned or discharged and the pleadings amended. Under the 1993 Rules, the period for adjustment is limited, but a party may still attempt to amend. It would appear that the practice of amending after the options hearing is becoming more widespread – at least in some sheriff courts. One sheriff has commented:

A guess – educated perhaps – suggests that no case ever comes to proof now without at least one minute of amendment. Indeed it is not unusual to be met at proof with a pile of papers which includes the third amended closed record. One of the consequences of the new rules has been a greater reliance on amendment and amendment procedure. (Johnston 1997: 4–5).

Morris and Headrick (1995: 14) found that sheriffs would sometimes permit repeated adjustment on the continued adjustment roll under the old procedure because they appreciated that to close the record when parties had not completed adjustment to their satisfaction only resulted in the problem of further alteration being taken to the amendment stage, which resulted in considerable additional expense.

It may be that the imposition of time-limited adjustment by the 1993 Rules has resulted in the increasing use of amendment which ultimately usurps the court's interventionist management function at the options hearing and authoritative guidance is still required as to whether the sheriff retains similar powers in relation to a rule 18.3 hearing on minutes of amendment and answers. It could be argued that the limiting of adjustment has resulted in problem displacement – delays now build up after the options hearing before the case reaches final adjudication.

Sanctions for Default

A significant problem for sheriffs has been selecting an appropriate sanction, if any, to apply to parties who have defaulted. This has been particularly so where the pursuer has failed to lodge a record for the options hearing. It is a matter for the sheriff's discretion. The 'hard' interpretation would suggest that the sheriff should dismiss the action unless persuasive reasons or the 'interests of justice' dictate that he exercises his dispensing power. However, the counter argument is that if the rules were partly designed to reduce delay and expense for litigants, adopting such a course does not necessarily achieve that objective. Such considerations informed the 'lenient' interpretation of the rules. If the action is dismissed the pursuer has expenses awarded against him. Further, an award of expenses as a sanction will often be ultimately relayed to the party unless the solicitor is found personally liable in the expense occasioned by the default, or he undertakes to pay the expenses awarded against his client.

Prior to the 1993 Rules, in considering an adverse award of expenses for procedural default, the court would often give consideration to the question of whether the conduct resulting in the default was that of the party or the solicitor. In considering decree of dismissal by default, it was usually considered inappropriate if there had been no default on the part of the litigant himself (Macphail 1987: 5–112; 14–08, 14–09). Although the cases following the 1993 Rules have considered that prejudice to the court is a consideration it is suggested that some sheriffs are reluctant to indirectly penalise the party nor directly penalise the agent. No distinction has been drawn in the case law between the actings of a pursuer and the actings (or lack of them) of his agent although this distinction has been drawn regarding the converse situation with defenders (*Ellis v Amec Offshore Developments Ltd* 1996 S.C.L.R. 403).

Conclusion

Due to the unavailability of published research into the operation of the 1993 Rules, the conclusions articulated in this paper are necessarily premissed on the observations of practitioners published in the literature, the writer's research and observations and anecdotal evidence. One may induce, however that the 1993 Rules have been only partially successful in obtaining the five policy objectives of the Sheriff Court Rules Council. Mays (1997) has suggested that old attitudes and approaches are accommodated in the new rules. It is submitted that he is correct. The 1993 Rules attempted to revolutionise the conduct of litigation in the sheriff's ordinary court. However, revolutions tend to return to an old order if they do not have the support of the majority. As Main and Wadia have argued, changes to systems of civil justice are dependent on the reaction of the culture they seek to alter. Cultures alter gradually and it was perhaps optimistic to expect that among practitioners, a Damascene attitudinal conversion would follow the implementation of rules. Those responsible for enforcing the Rules, however, initially took a firm line. Just as revolutions can be sustained by force, by and large, sheriffs and Sheriffs Principal considered that they had a responsibility to make the 1993 Rules work in practice. The strict approach elucidated through case law during the year following the introduction of the 1993 Rules was a radical departure from the pre-1993 position. As Foulis has noted, prior to implementation, practitioners probably did not anticipate the consequences of their failure to comply with the time limits imposed by the rules. However, the sanctions for non-compliance imposed by the courts in terms of the strict approach were not designed to punish or stimulate solicitors to improve their performance by a system of reward and punishment. Although sheriffs had been enjoined to take a firm approach to sanctioning non-compliance prior to the rules coming into force, the 'hard approach' (e.g. by dismissing cases) was said to be part of the duty of the court to do justice between the parties, (Sheriff Principal Risk Q.C.: 1996 S.C.L.R. 'Quotations' 1173B). In accordance with previous theory, the courts did not exist and had never existed for the sake of discipline (Macphail 1987: 15–114). The courts have continued to maintain that the strict approach should not employed to cut the Gordian knot.

Although the 'strict' approach came to be acknowledged as the proper approach to be employed, it is uncertain to what extent it was and is universally applied in practice. If the strict approach is being eroded in practice by aberrations in procedure and 'mischievous' interpretations of the 1993 Rules, this should be having an effect on 'access to justice'. Assuming the 1993 Rules expedite cases on route to adjudication or settlement and delay and expense is reduced, then superficially there has been increased access to justice. However, if sheriffs view their expeditious powers 'mischievously' as opposed to 'literally', whilst the instant interests of substantive justice may be served, does arising inconsistency in approach lead to a lack of predictability and Sheriff Johnston's 'know your sheriff' argument? Any system of justice must be clear and predictable, procedural justice included. Balancing these considerations will always be problematic. The scope for inconsistency has increased in line with increased discretion. There are multifarious interpretations of the 'expedition of the cause'.

If inconsistency in approach is an unwelcome element in sheriff court civil practice, a solution may be lie with sheriffs receiving additional training as to the exercise of the pro-active power. There are two problems with this however. Firstly, it might be perceived as curbing traditional judicial independence and secondly, more fundamentally, it is extremely difficult to give guidance as to the exercise of discretion and pro-activity. They are inherently substantive. It may be a solution can be found by the new Judicial Studies Committee.

There is also uncertainty as to the current attitude of practitioners to the 1993 Rules. Although there was an initial scepticism and perception that the procedure had not required alteration, it is difficult to assess whether the rules are now accepted and complied with as envisaged by the Rules Council. The number of cases appealed has dropped drastically which might indicate that this is so. However, observations by the writer and articles by the profession in the literature seem to indicate that practitioners have devised methods of avoiding, for whatever reason, the most draconian interventionist aspects of the rules. There would appear to be increased use of minutes of amendment on route to final determination. Adjustments are intimated immediately prior to or on the last day permitted for adjustment. Motions are made for innovative steps in procedure. Whilst these approaches may not be calculated to delay final resolution, very often that is their effect. In addition, before the introduction of the 1993 Rules, solicitors were urged to use the procedures to compel their opponents to meet their case (Neilson 1993: 426). This would not appear to have happened. As Sheriff Johnston has remarked, solicitors are 'extremely forbearing with their colleagues' and are reluctant to do so. If the writer's propositions are correct, the initial hostility found within some elements of the profession would be expected to abate if methods are now used to wrest from the court some control over the progress of litigation.

The 1993 Rules have been in existence now for nearly four years and have been subsequently amended twice. The amendments have been primarily clarificatory (dealing with anomalies raised in case law) and corrective (spelling mistakes etc.) (although changes were made to motion procedure). The thrust of the 1993 Rules has remained unaltered and by inference the Sheriff Court Rules Council would appear satisfied that they are working in practice. The perception amongst Sheriffs Principal, sheriffs and court staff would appear to be that the rules have been a success 'on the whole' and in any event a considerable improvement on their predecessors.

Surrendering the progress of litigation to the control of the court may be seen as a potential solution to the interminable problems of delay which have traditionally been found in Scottish civil procedure. However, as sheriff court procedure has shown, there are inherent difficulties with the exercise of judicial inquisitorial powers. Lord Cullen's proposals for reform of the Court of Session incorporate powers of judicial interventionism which go beyond that which has been tried in the sheriff court. The Faculty of Advocates has expressed reservations preferring the retention of the traditional judicial role. If Lord Cullen's proposals are to operate as envisaged, the Court of Session may look to lessons that are being learned in the sheriff court. Current proposals for reform of civil procedure in the Court of Session will be dependent for their success on a number of factors. Firstly, if the culture of reception is wholly or in part hostile to the proposed reform, then the likelihood of successful implementation is diminished. If those practising under new rules are not fully agreeable to them, mechanisms will be devised and tried in an attempt to undermine the effectiveness of reforms and to return to the old order. The history of civil procedure is littered with similar examples. Secondly, (a point acknowledged by Lord Cullen), the judiciary must be fully supportive of any proposals that are implemented. If aberration or innovation is condoned, the interests of natural justice entail universal application in all similar cases. This will invariably result in a decrease in efficacy. Thirdly, pro-active powers, increased judicial discretion and interventionism may be useful in the expedition of cases through the courts and a reduction in expense and delay, but if these powers are exercised inconsistently, the end result may be decreased predictability and a diminution in the coherence of the civil justice system as a whole. Fourthly, the traditional safety net of appeal is compromised by the very nature of the exercise of discretion. The appellate courts have traditionally been reluctant to intervene with the exercise of judicial discretion. Fifthly, it is difficult to give guidance to the judiciary as to the exercise of powers designed to progress actions through the courts. The exercise of these powers will always be dependent on substantive considerations and may ultimately be seen as a threat to judicial independence.

The argument that the introduction of case management and increased judicial discretion is the solution to the problems of delay and expense would appear to have gained credence in recent years. Any civil justice system will involve some delay and will involve some complexity. This does not mean that better systems of civil justice cannot be devised. However, altering the roles of parties and judges and incorporating elements of foreign procedure in the face of indigenous scepticism is not necessarily the panacean solution. If the propositions expounded in this article are correct, the sheriff court has shown that there are problems with such an approach. The Court of Session, the profession and all those interested in the future of civil procedure in Scotland should look to and learn from lessons currently being learned following the introduction of 1993 Rules in the sheriff court.

Cases referred to:

Burtonport Fishermen's Co-operative v. Sans Unkles 1994 S.C.L.R. 844
Strathclyde Business Park (Management) Ltd v. Cochrane 1995 S.L.T. (Sh Ct) 69
Welsh v. Thornhome Services and Ors. 1994 S.C.L.R. 1021
Ritchie v. Maersk 1994 S.C.L.R. 1038
Mahoney v. Officer 1995 S.L.T. (Sh Ct) 49; 1994 S.C.L.R. 1059
Morran v. Glasgow Council of Tenants' Associations 1995 S.L.T. (Sh Ct) 46; 1994 S.C.L.R 1065
Price v. Fernando 1995 S.C.L.R. 23

Group 4 Total Security Ltd. v. Jaymarke Developments Ltd. 1996 S.L.T. (Sh Ct) 61; 1995 S.C.L.R. 303
D.T.Z. Debenham Thorpe v. Henderson Transport 1995 S.L.T. 553; 1995 S.C.L.R. 345
De Melo v. Bazazi 1995 S.L.T. (Sh Ct) 57; 1995 S.C.L.R. 564
D.A. Baird v. Nisbet & Anr 1995 S.C.L.R. 1127
Ellis v. Amec Offshore Developments Ltd. 1996 S.C.L.R. 403
Dinardo Partnership v. Thomas Tait & Sons 1995 S.C.L.R. (Sh. Ct) 941
Bryson v. Gresham 1996 S.C.L.R. 776

Bibliography

Black, R., (1982). *An Introduction to Written Pleadings*. Law Society of Scotland: Edinburgh.
Cairns, B. C., (1994). Managing Civil Litigation: An Australian Adaption of American Experience. *Civil Justice Quarterly*; 50–70.
Cullen, The Hon. Lord, (1995). *Review of the Business of the Outer House of the Court of Session*. Scottish Courts Administration: Edinburgh.
Dailly, M., (1993). Drastic reduction in sheriff court delays expected. *SCOLAG*, December; 180–182.
Deutsch, A., (1995). The Settlement That Never Was. *Civil Practice Bulletin* **5**; 4–5.
Deutsch, A., (1996). Two Gripes from the Sheriff Court. *Civil Practice Bulletin* **10**; 8–9.
Edinburgh Bar Association, (1995). *Recommendations of Edinburgh Bar Association for Changes to the Sheriff Court Ordinary Cause Rules*, as established by the Act of Sederunt (Sheriff Court Ordinary Cause Rules) 1993.
Foulis, L., (1996a). Sheriff Court Practice – Three Years of the New Rules. *The Journal of the Law Society of Scotland* **41**; 438–441.
Foulis, L., (1996b). Sheriff Court Rules Changes. *The Journal of the Law Society of Scotland*, **41**; 491–494.
Foulis, L., (1997) Sheriff Court Practice – Recent Decisions in Civil Procedures. *The Journal of the Law Society of Scotland*, **42**; 148–151.
Gill, The Hon Lord, (1995). *The Case for a Civil Justice Review. The Journal of the Law Society of Scotland* **40**; 129–133.
Grant Report, (1967). *The Sheriff Court; Report by the Committee appointed by the Secretary of State for Scotland*. Cmnd 3248, HMSO.
Hansard, (1994). Lord Morton of Shuna. Parliamentary Debates, House of Lords, *Hansard* **1614**; 181–184.
Hughes Commission, (1980). *Royal Commission on Legal Services in Scotland*. Cmnd 7846 HMSO.
Jacob, J. I .H., (1987). *The Fabric of English Civil Justice*. The Hamlyn Lectures. London: Stevens and Sons.
John Wheatley Centre, (1997). *Scots Law and the Scottish Parliament*. The Governance of Scotland Project.
Johnston, A. G., (1995a). Options Hearings – A View From Glasgow. *Civil Practice Bulletin*, **1**; 5–7.
Johnston, A. G., (1995b). A Sheriff in Woolf's Clothing. *Civil Practice Bulletin* **4**; 4–5.
Johnston, A. G., (1995c). The Options Roll Revisited. *Civil Practice Bulletin* **6**; 5–6.
Johnston, A. G., (1996). Miscellaneous Procedure Roll. *Civil Practice Bulletin* **9**; 6–7.
Johnston, A. G., (1997). Procedurally – Does the End Justify the Means? *Civil Practice Bulletin*, **14**; 4–5.

Jolowicz, J. A., (1996). The Woolf Report and the Adversary System. *Civil Justice Quarterly* **15**; 198–210.
Kelbie, D., (1995). Options Hearings – A View From Aberdeen. *Civil Practice Bulletin* **1**; 7–9.
Lewis, W. J., (1939). *Sheriff Court Practice.* 8th edition. Edinburgh: W. Green and Son, Ltd.
McCulloch, W., and Laing, E., (1995). *New Ordinary Cause Rules.* Great Britain: CLT Professional Publishing.
Macphail, I. R., (1988). *Sheriff Court Practice.* Edinburgh: SULI/W. Green and Sons.
Marshall, T., (1997). Appeals, Corrections and the Dispensing Power. *Civil Practice Bulletin,* **15**; 2–5.
Mays, R., (1997). Frying Pan, Fire or Melting Pot? – Reforming Scottish Civil Justice in the 1990s. *Juridical Review,* **2**; 91–109.
Morris, S. and Headrick, D., (1995). *Pilgrim's Process? Defended Actions in the Sheriff's Ordinary Court.* Central Research Unit, The Scottish Office.
Morrison, N .M. P., (1995). Editorial. *Civil Practice Bulletin* **4**; 1–2.
Morrison, N. M. P., (1996). The Cullen Report. *Scots Law Times* (News); 93–100.
Morton, The Hon. Lord, (1995). Procedural Reform of the Court of Session. *Civil Practice Bulletin,* **1**; 2–3.
Neilson, H., (1993). Sheriff Court Options Hearings Beware the Ides of March. *The Journal of the Law Society of Scotland,* **38**; 425–426.
Neilson, H., (1996). *Written Pleadings and the New Sheriff Court Rules.* Legal Services Agency; Seminar on Written Pleadings in the Sheriff Court, Glasgow, 12th February 1996.
Scottish Courts Administration, (1996) *Civil Judicial Statistics Scotland 1995.* HMSO, Edinburgh
Sheriff Court Rules Council, (1990). *Consultation Paper*; Review of Sheriff Civil Court Procedures and Practices.
Sheriff Court Rules Council, (1991). *Report on Proposals for New Procedures for Defended Ordinary Causes and Defended Family Actions*; Review of Sheriff Civil Court Procedures and Practices.
Stevenson, A. G., (1996). Ascertaining Disputed Matters at an Options Hearing. *Civil Practice Bulletin* **10**; 6–7.
The Herald, (1996). *Cash plea to oil the wheels of civil justice.* 17th Jan. 1996.
The Scotsman, (1997) *The price paid for justice.* Editorial comment. 1st April 1997.
Upton, M., (1996). The Cullen Review. *The Journal of the Law Society of Scotland* **41**; 111–117.
Vocational Training Unit, (1995). Handout *Civil Court Procedure: Is the Dust Settling?* University of Aberdeen.
Walker, D. M., (1992). *The Scottish Legal System.* 7th edition, Edinburgh: W. Green /Sweet and Maxwell.
White, D., (1994). *Sheriff's Ordinary Court Practice & Procedure.* 2nd edition. Great Britain: Tolley.
Woolman, S., (1996). *'Pleadings'; Scots Law into the 21st Century.* MacQueen H. L., (ed). Edinburgh: W. Green/Sweet & Maxwell; 277–283.
Zander, M., (1997). The Woolf Report: Forwards or Backwards for the New Lord Chancellor? *Civil Justice Quarterly* **16**; 208–227.
Zuckermann, A. A. S., and Cranston, R., (1995). *Reform of Civil Procedure, Essays on 'Access to Justice'.* Oxford: Oxford University. Zander, M., Caseflow Management in the Trial Court; 1–30; Why Lord Woolf's Proposed Reforms of Civil Litigation Should be Rejected; 79–96.